# Catering costs and control

*To my husband and daughter*

# Catering costs and control

*Grace Paige*

Cassell · London

CASSELL LTD.
35 Red Lion Square, London WC1R 4SG
and at Sydney, Auckland, Toronto, Johannesburg
An affiliate of Macmillan Publishing Co. Inc., New York

First published 1977
Second impression 1978
Third impression 1979
Fourth impression 1981

I.S.B.N. 0 304 29758 5

Printed and bound in Great Britain at
The Camelot Press Ltd, Southampton

# Preface

When people decide to start in business for themselves, they may have to withdraw their savings from the bank, which is paying them a regular rate of interest, or they may decide to borrow the money from a bank or some other source and have to pay interest. It may also mean giving up a job and a regular wage in order to devote themselves to the business. It is common sense, therefore, that the business will have to yield sufficient income to cover the material cost of the goods they produce, plus the labour costs of producing the goods and the expenses of running the business, such as heat, light, telephone and other sundry expenses. It must also provide a net profit which is at least equal to the loss of wages and the interest that has been lost by taking the money out of the bank, or the interest which has to be paid for borrowing the money. Similarly an investor or shareholder in a company is also risking his capital in a business, so he too has the right to expect a fair return on the capital invested by way of dividends (share of the profits) from the company.

Many people engaged in the hotel and catering industry seem to be of the opinion that costing and cost control systems are only necessary in large companies; on the contrary, no matter how small an establishment, a system of costing and control is an important aid to efficient management and essential if profitability is to be ensured. In the hospitality industry, as in every other industry, the keen competition which prevails makes it necessary for the businessman to keep accurate and systematic records of the actual cost of the goods and services that he sells.

Some industries have developed highly sophisticated methods of cost control, understandable only to the higher echelons of executives, but if a business is to be really successful and attain maximum profitability, every single member of staff should be cost-conscious, and it is the responsibility of executives, heads of department and supervisors to instruct their staff and ensure that they are aware of the purpose and value of costing and cost control, for investigation has proved that one of the major causes of failure in the catering industry has been lack of understanding of and failure to implement cost control systems.

The following chapters are designed to illustrate the basic principles involved in food costing and cost control and to show how all operational information relating to the establishment is used to promote effective and profitable management decisions.

The aim of this book has been to provide a practical text for entrants to the hotel and catering industry and for students studying for examinations of the City & Guilds of London Institute, the Ordinary National Diploma in Hotel and Catering Operations and Membership Examinations of the Hotel, Catering and Institutional Management Association.

It is also hoped that this book will provide basic information which will be useful to practising caterers and hotel-keepers on the principles underlying food costing and cost control and illustrate how all operational information relating to the establishment can be used to promote cost consciousness and effective and profitable management decisions.

# Contents

Preface     5

PART 1—FOOD COSTING

1    **Weights and Measures**     10
Notation. The metric system. Costing calculations. Averages of weights. Mixtures and blends. PROGRESS TEST QUESTIONS

2    **The Basic Elements of Cost**     24
Basic elements of cost. Different types of establishment. Turnover and profit margins. Materials (food cost). Staff meals. Monthly comparative percentage statements. Catering returns. PROGRESS TEST QUESTIONS

3    **Calculation of Selling Prices**     35
Portion control. Calculation of selling prices (mark-up, gross profit margins and gross profit). Pricing policy. PROGRESS TEST QUESTIONS

4    **Unit and Multiple Costing**     49
The recipe manual. Unit costing. Menu costing, Special functions. PROGRESS TEST QUESTIONS

5    **Meat costing**     66
Meat costing. Wholesale cuts. Bone and cooking loss. Cooked meat price. PROGRESS TEST QUESTIONS

PART 2—AREAS OF CONTROL

6    **Cost Control**     79
The objects and advantages of cost control. The implementation of control. Areas of control. The control pattern. Control as an effective aid to management. PROGRESS TEST QUESTIONS

7    **Food Control**     88
The stock control system. Duties and responsibilities of the storekeeper. Documents used in control of ordering. Stock control. Stock checks. Purchasing. Stock valuation. Discounts. PROGRESS TEST QUESTIONS

8  **Kitchen Control**                                                  107
   Duties of the *chef de cuisine*. Kitchen percentages. Staff meals.
   Control of issues. Centralised production kitchens. Catering
   results. Fraud in the kitchen. PROGRESS TEST QUESTIONS

9  **Wines, Spirits and Beer Control**                                  125
   Cost control pattern. Purchasing. Receiving goods. Cellar
   procedures. Fixed bars. Control of bar stock at selling price.
   Calculation of gross profit on bars. Stocktaking and stock
   checks. Frauds in bars. PROGRESS TEST QUESTIONS

10 **Cash Control**                                                     145
   Sales recorded through tills. Credit sales—room service. Cash
   and credit sales in the restaurant. Value Added Tax. Cheques.
   Credit cards. Cash floats. Petty cash control. Mechanised
   accounting. PROGRESS TEST QUESTIONS

PART 3—BUDGETARY CONTROL

11 **Cost Concepts**                                                    165
   Nature and behaviour of costs. Unit costs. Break-even point.
   Marginal cost. Apportionment of costs. Calculations of
   charges. PROGRESS TEST QUESTIONS

12 **Budgetary Control**                                                181
   Objects and advantages. The budget committee. The budget
   period. Types of budget. Development of budgets. Limiting
   factors. Pricing policy. PROGRESS TEST QUESTIONS

13 **Financial Budgets**                                                189
   Profits budgets. Capital budgets. Cash budgets. Cash flow
   statement. Operating statements. PROGRESS TEST QUESTIONS

14 **Operating Budgets**                                                204
   The sales budget. Determination of sales targets. Labour cost
   budget. Overheads cost budget. Housekeeping budget.
   Maintenance budget. PROGRESS TEST QUESTIONS

15 **Industrial Catering**                                              215
   Canteens and subsidies. Airline catering. Ships catering.
   School meal catering. Hospital catering. PROGRESS TEST
   QUESTIONS

# Part One

# Food Costing

# CHAPTER 1

# Weights and Measures

## Notation

In order to minimise the possibility of error when costing it is important that the correct standardised notation is used as follows:

*Amounts*

| | | | |
|---|---|---|---|
| Whole pounds | £3 | written as | £3·00 |
| Pence | 57p | ,, | £0·57 |
| One penny | 1p | ,, | £0·01 |
| One quarter of a penny | $\frac{1}{4}$p | ,, | £0·0025 |
| One half of a penny | $\frac{1}{2}$p | ,, | £0·005 |
| Three-quarters of a penny | $\frac{3}{4}$p | ,, | £0·0075 |
| Decimal fraction of a penny, e.g. | 3/10p | ,, | £0·003 |
| Mixed amount | £39·15$\frac{1}{2}$ | ,, | £39·155 |

*Measures of number*

| | | |
|---|---|---|
| 1 dozen | = | 12 units |
| 1 score | = | 20 units |
| 1 gross | = | 144 units |
| 1 quire | = | 24 sheets of paper |
| 1 ream | = | 20 quires of paper (480 sheets) |
| 1 bale | = | 10 reams |

The prices used in the calculations in this chapter should not be regarded as indicative of current prices of commodities; these can fluctuate daily. The examples are merely intended to illustrate the theory of the costing involved.

It is important when costing to calculate to at least three decimal places, and in large-scale catering to at least five decimal places, for if, for instance, an item was undercosted by 0·003p the resulting loss would be 0·3p on 100 items, and 3p on 1,000 items, and if 100 million items were produced annually the loss would be £3,000 per year. It must be appreciated that food is a perishable commodity that can result in loss through wastage or spoilage, and therefore it is always advisable to round up to the nearest unit above when costing to allow for any loss, rather than round down.

Before an approach to food costing can be made a sound knowledge of weights, measures and catering and food pack sizes is necessary. The ability to do rapid basic calculations should also be developed as ready reckoners and calculators are not always to hand.

Great Britain and many other countries of the world have always used the *Imperial* system of weights and measures as follows:

*Avoirdupois table (dry weight)*

| | | |
|---|---|---|
| 16 drams | = | 1 oz |
| 16 ounces (oz) | = | 1 pound (1 lb) |
| 14 pounds | = | 1 stone (st) |
| 2 stones (28 lb) | = | 1 quarter (qr) |
| 4 quarters (112 lb) | = | 1 hundredweight (cwt) |
| 20 cwt (2,240 lb) | = | 1 ton |

*Liquid measure*

| | | |
|---|---|---|
| 8 drams | = | 1 fluid oz |
| 5 fluid oz | = | 1 gill (40 drams) |
| 4 gills | = | 1 pint |
| 20 fluid oz | = | 1 pint |
| 2 pints | = | 1 quart |
| 4 quarts | = | 1 gallon |

*Ale and beer measure*

| | | |
|---|---|---|
| $4\frac{1}{2}$ gallons | = | 1 pin (20·457 litres) |
| 9 gallons | = | 1 firkin (40·914 litres) |
| 10 gallons | = | 1 keg (45·46 litres) |
| 18 gallons | = | 1 kilderkin (81·828 litres) |
| 36 gallons | = | 1 barrel (163·656 litres) |
| 54 gallons | = | 1 hogshead (245·484 litres) |

*Long measure*

| | | |
|---|---|---|
| 12 inches | = | 1 foot |
| 3 feet | = | 1 yard |
| 1,760 yards | = | 1 mile |

# The metric system

The metric system, which is in use throughout the world, is a decimal system which works in multiples of ten and has proved to be simpler and superior to the 'Imperial' system of weights and measures. Therefore it is logical to assume that in time it will become the only system used throughout the world. Great Britain is already in the transition stage and many industries have already adopted the metric system. Each denomination in the metric system is one-tenth of the one above it and ten times the one below it. These Tables should be memorised:

*Multiplying prefixes*

| | | |
|---|---|---|
| kilo- (k) | = | 1,000 units |
| *hekto- (h) | = | 100 units |
| *deka- (da) | = | 10 units |
| unit (gramme, metre, litre) | = | 1 unit |
| deci- (d) | = | 1/10 or 0·1 unit |
| centi- (c) | = | 1/100 or 0·01 unit |
| milli- (m) | = | 1/1,000 or 0·001 unit |

The *gramme* is the unit of weight; hence:

| | | |
|---|---|---|
| 1 kilogramme (kg) | = | 1,000 grammes (or 10 hg) |
| 1 hektogramme (hg) | = | 100 grammes (or 10 dag) |
| *1 dekagramme (dag) | = | 10 grammes |
| unit (g) | = | 1 gramme |
| *1 decigramme (dg) | = | 1/10 or 0·1 gramme |
| 1 centigramme (cg) | = | 1/100 or 0·1 gramme |
| 1 milligramme (mg) | = | 1/1,000 or 0·001 gramme |

The *litre* is the unit of capacity, hence:

| | | |
|---|---|---|
| *1 kilolitre (kl) | = | 1,000 litres (or 10 hl) = 1 cubic metre |
| *1 hektolitre (hl) | = | 100 litres (or 10 dal) |
| *1 dekalitre (dal) | = | 10 litres |
| unit (litre) | = | 1 litre = 1 cubic decimetre |
| *1 decilitre (dl) | = | 1/10 or 0·1 litre |
| 1 centilitre (cl) | = | 1/100 or 0·01 litre |
| 1 millilitre (ml) | = | 1/1,000 or 0·001 litre = 1 cubic centimetre |

The *metre* is the unit of length, hence:

| | | |
|---|---|---|
| 1 kilometre (km) | = | 1,000 metres (or 10 hm) |
| *1 hectometre (hm) | = | 100 metres (or 10 dm) |
| *1 dekametre (dam) | = | 10 metres |
| unit (m) | = | 1 metre |
| 1 decimetre (dm) | = | 1/10 or 0·1 metre |
| 1 centimetre (cm) | = | 1/100 or 0·01 metre |
| 1 millimetre (mm) | = | 1/1,000 or 0·001 metre |

Because the system works in multiples of ten, moving the decimal point 1 place to the left divides by 10, 2 places divides by 100 and 3 places to the left divides by 1,000. Thus to express grammes as kilograms, divide by 1,000:

*Example:* 2,000 g = 2 kg
1,500 g = 1·5 kg
1,250 g = 1·25 kg

---

* Seldom encountered in practice.

To express centigrammes in grammes, divide by 100 by moving the decimal point 2 places to the left:

*Example:* 2,000 cg = 20 g
1,500 cg = 15 g
1,250 cg = 12·5 g

To express milligrammes in grammes divide by 1,000 by moving the decimal point 3 places to the left:

*Example:* 1,250 mg = 1·25 g
12,500 mg = 12·5 g
125,000 mg = 125 g

To convert from larger to smaller units, multiply instead of divide by moving the decimal point: 1 place to right to multiply by 10; 2 places to multiply by 100; and 3 places to right to multiply by 1,000:

*Example:* 1·5 kg = 15 hg        15,000 dg
150 dag       150,000 cg
1,500 g       1,500,000 mg

The following tables show the relationship between certain Imperial and metric measures; until the metric system has been fully adopted it would be well to keep the equivalents in mind.

**Weight**—Kilogramme = 1,000 grammes = 2 lb 3·27 oz

| Metric | Imperial approx. | exact |
|---|---|---|
| 1 g | 1/30 oz | 0·035 oz |
| 5 g | 1/6 oz | 0·176 oz |
| 10 g | ⅓ oz | 0·353 oz |
| 20 g | ¾ oz | 0·705 oz |
| 30 g | 1 oz | 1·058 oz |
| 50 g | 1¾ oz | 1·763 oz |
| 100 g | 3½ oz | 3·527 oz |
| 250 g (¼ kg) | 9 oz | 8·818 oz |
| 500 g (½ kg) | 1 lb 2 oz | 17·637 oz |
| 750 g (¾ kg) | 1 lb 10 oz | 26·456 oz |
| 1,000 g (1 kg) | 2 lb 4 oz | 35·274 oz |

**Liquids**—litre = 10 decilitres = 1,000 millilitres = 1·76 pints

| | | |
|---|---|---|
| ¼ decilitre (dl) | 1 fl oz | 0·88 fl oz |
| ½ dl | 1¾ fl oz | 1·76 fl oz |
| ¾ dl | 2½ fl oz | 2·64 fl oz |
| 1 dl | 3½ fl oz | 3·52 fl oz |
| ¼ litre | 9 fl oz | 8·80 fl oz |
| ½ litre | 18 fl oz | 17·60 fl oz |

| $\frac{3}{4}$ litre | $1\frac{1}{3}$ pints | 26·40 fl oz |
|---|---|---|
| 1 litre | $1\frac{3}{4}$ pints | 35·20 fl oz |
| 5 litres | $8\frac{3}{4}$ pints | 176·00 fl oz |

## Useful equivalents

| | approx. | exact |
|---|---|---|
| 1 oz | 30 g | 28·3 g |
| 2 oz | 60 g | 56·7 g |
| 4 oz | 115 g | 113·4 g |
| 6 oz | 170 g | 170·1 g |
| 8 oz | 225 g | 226·8 g |
| 12 oz | 340 g | 340·2 g |
| 1 lb | 450 g | 0·454 kg |
| 1 stone | 6 kg | 6·35 kg |
| 1 cwt | 50 kg | 50·80 kg |
| $\frac{1}{2}$ gill | $\frac{1}{16}$ litre | 0·071 litre |
| 1 gill | $\frac{1}{8}$ litre | 0·142 litre |
| $\frac{3}{8}$ pint | $\frac{1}{5}$ litre | 0·213 litre |
| 1 pint | $\frac{1}{2}$ litre | 0·568 litre |
| 1 quart | 1 litre | 1·136 litres |
| 1 gallon | $4\frac{1}{2}$ litres | 4·546 litres |

**Length**—1 metre=100 centimetres=1,000 millimetres=39·37 inches

| Metric | Imperial approx. | exact |
|---|---|---|
| 1 mm | 1/25 inch | 0·039 inch |
| 2 mm | 1/12 inch | 0·079 inch |
| 5 mm | $\frac{1}{5}$ inch | 0·197 inch |
| 1 cm | $\frac{2}{5}$ inch | 0·394 inch |
| 5 cm | 2 inches | 1·97 inches |
| 10 cm | 4 inches | 3·94 inches |
| 20 cm | 8 inches | 7·87 inches |
| 50 cm | 20 inches | 19·68 inches |
| 1 m | $3\frac{1}{4}$ feet | 39·37 inches |

## Useful Equivalents

| | approx. | exact |
|---|---|---|
| $\frac{1}{8}$ inch | 3 mm | 3·175 mm |
| $\frac{1}{4}$ inch | $\frac{1}{2}$ cm | 0·635 cm |
| $\frac{1}{2}$ inch | 1 cm | 1·27 cm |
| 1 foot | 3 dm | 3·05 dm |

15

**Oven Temperatures**

| Gas Regulo number | Celsius (Centigrade) (°C) | Fahrenheit (°F) | |
|---|---|---|---|
| $\frac{1}{2}$ | 120 | 250 | very cool |
| 1 | 135 | 275 | cool |
| 2 | 150 | 300 | warm |
| 3 | 160 | 325 | moderate |
| 4 | 175 | 350 | moderate |
| 5 | 190 | 375 | moderately hot |
| 6 | 205 | 400 | hot |
| 7 | 220 | 425 | hot |
| 8 | 230 | 450 | very hot |
| 9 | 245 | 475 | very hot |

*Example 1:* Convert 4 kilogrammes to pounds:

1 kg = 2·2 lb

∴ 4 kg = 2·2 × 4 = 8·8 lb (approx. 8 lb 13 oz)

*Example 2:* Convert 10·75 kilogrammes to pounds:

$$
\begin{array}{r}
10 \cdot 75 \\
\times 2 \cdot 2 \\
\hline
21 \cdot 50 \\
2 \cdot 15 \\
\hline
23 \cdot 65
\end{array}
$$
pounds (23 lb 10$\frac{1}{2}$ oz approx.)

*Example 3:* Convert 100 litres to gallons:

1 litre = 1·76 pints

100 litres = 176 pints = 22 gallons

*Example 4:* The following recipe was issued using the metric system. Convert it to Imperial measures.

*Savarin (2 rings—16 portions)*

| | Imperial approx. |
|---|---|
| 480 g Flour | 1 lb |
| 180 g Butter | 6 oz |
| 30 g Sugar | 1 oz |
| 6 Eggs | 6 |
| 15 g Salt | $\frac{1}{2}$ oz |
| 20 g Yeast | $\frac{5}{8}$ oz |
| $\frac{1}{8}$ l Milk | 1 gill |

*Example* 5 : Convert and cost the following order : (Calculation on approx. equivalents)

| | Approx. equivalent | Cost £ |
|---|---|---|
| 33 lb of Potatoes @ 16p per kilo | 15 kg | 2·40 |
| ¾ lb of Ham @ £1·58 per kilo | 360 g | 0·57 |
| 3½ gallons of milk @ 11p per litre | 17½ litres | 1·92 |
| | | **£4·89** |

Compare the difference in cost when calculating on actual equivalents :

33 lb Potatoes @ 16p per kilo = 0·454 kg

$$\begin{array}{r} 0·454 \\ \times 33 \\ \hline 13,620 \\ 1,362 \\ \hline 14·982 \text{ kilos @ 16p per lb.} \\ \times 16 \\ \hline 149,820 \\ 89,892 \\ \hline 2·39712 \quad (£2·40) \end{array}$$

¾ of ham @ £1·58 per kilo

$$\begin{array}{l} 1 \text{ lb} = 0·454 \text{ kilo} \\ \tfrac{1}{2} \text{ lb} = 0·227 \\ \tfrac{1}{4} \text{ lb} = 0·1135 \\ \tfrac{5}{8} \text{ lb} = 0·3405 \text{ kilo} \end{array}$$

$$\therefore \frac{340·5 \text{ g} \times £1·58}{1,000} = 53·8\text{p} \quad (54\text{p})$$

3½ gallons milk @ 11p per litre

$$\begin{array}{l} 1 \text{ gallon} = 4·543 \text{ litres} \\ 3 \text{ gallons} = 13·629 \\ \tfrac{1}{2} \text{ gallon} = 2·271 \\ \hline 15·900 \text{ litres} \end{array}$$

15·9 litres @ 11p per litre = £1·75

It is never advisable to cost on approximate equivalents, for as you can see from the foregoing comparisons, it could result in sizeable discrepancies over large quantities; and unrealistic figures could be to the caterer's disadvantage.

# Costing calculations

*Example 1:*
Find the cost of a piece of cheese weighing 1·5 kg at 96p per kilo:

$$
\begin{array}{rl}
& \pounds \\
1 \text{ kilo} = & 0\cdot96 \\
\tfrac{1}{2}\text{ kilo} = & 0\cdot48 \\
\hline
& \underline{\underline{\pounds 1\cdot44}}
\end{array}
$$

*Example 2:*
Find the cost of a joint of meat weighing 4·25 kg at £1·44 per kilo:

$$
\begin{array}{rl}
& \pounds \\
4 \text{ kilos} = & 5\cdot76 \\
\tfrac{1}{4}\text{ kilo} = & 0\cdot36 \\
\hline
& \underline{\underline{\pounds 6\cdot12}}
\end{array}
$$

*Example 3:*
Find the cost of a joint of bacon weighing 1·15 kg at £1·36 per kilo:

*Method 1:*

$$
\begin{array}{rl}
& \pounds \\
1 \text{ kilo} = & 1\cdot36 \\
\dfrac{150 \text{ grammes}}{1{,}000} \times \pounds1\cdot36 = & 0\cdot204 \\
\hline
& \underline{\underline{\pounds 1\cdot564}} \text{ (say £1·57)}
\end{array}
$$

*Method 2:*
When multiplying by decimals, multiply as if by a whole number then count the figures behind the decimal point in both numbers; then count the same number to the left in the answer and place the decimal point, e.g.:

£1·36 multiplied by 1·15 kg.

$$
\begin{array}{r}
136 \times \\
115 \\
\hline
13600 \\
1360 \\
680 \\
\hline
1\cdot5640 \\
\end{array}
$$
(4 figures behind decimal point)

Answer £1·564 (say £1·57)

*Example 4:*

Four chickens costing 52p per kilo weighing:

|              | kg    |
|--------------|-------|
|              | 1·24  |
|              | 1·15  |
|              | 1·09  |
|              | 1·36  |
| Total weight | 4·84  |

*Cost:*
$$
\begin{array}{r}
484 \times \\
52 \\
\hline
24200 \\
968 \\
\hline
251 \cdot 68 \\
\end{array}
$$
(2 figures behind decimal point)

$= 251 \cdot 68\text{p}$  $= £2 \cdot 52$ to nearest penny

# Cost of quantities

Given the price for 50 kilogrammes, the prices for smaller quantities can be calculated by the 'practice method':

|                                    | £      |                                       |
|------------------------------------|--------|---------------------------------------|
| 50 kg cost                         | 12·00  |                                       |
| 5 kg cost                          | 1·20   | (move decimal point 1 place to left)  |
| 1 kg cost ($\frac{1}{5}$ of 5 kg)  | 0·24   |                                       |
| 100 g cost ($\frac{1}{10}$ of 1 kg)| 0·024  | (move decimal point 1 place to left)  |
| 50 g cost ($\frac{1}{2}$ above)    | 0·012  |                                       |
| 25 g cost ($\frac{1}{2}$ above)    | 0·006  |                                       |
| 500 g cost ($\frac{1}{2}$ of 1 kg) | 0·12   |                                       |
| 250 g cost ($\frac{1}{2}$ above)   | 0·06   |                                       |

*Example 1:*

If icing sugar is quoted at £9·50 per 50 kg, find the cost of 2·2 kg:

|              | £      |                           |
|--------------|--------|---------------------------|
| 50 kg cost   | 9·50   |                           |
| 10 kg cost   | 1·90   | (divide by 5)             |
| 2 kg cost    | 0·38   | (divide by 5)             |
| 1 kg cost    | 0·19   | ($\frac{1}{2}$ above)     |
| 200 g cost   | 0·038  | ($\frac{1}{5}$ of above)  |

*Cost:* 2·2 kg at £9·50 per 50 kg:

|          | £      |
|----------|--------|
| 2 kg =   | 0·38   |
| 200 g =  | 0·038  |
|          | £0·418 |

£0·418 (£0·42 to nearest penny)

The prices of some commodities such as eggs, oysters, cases of tinned foods are usually quoted by the dozen.

*Example 2:*
    Find the cost of 57 eggs at 32p per dozen:

$$
\begin{array}{lll}
& 57 & \qquad\pounds \\
\text{less} & \underline{48} = 4\,\text{doz at 32p} = & 1\cdot 28 \\
\text{leaves} & \underline{\phantom{0}9} & \\
& \phantom{0}6 = \tfrac{1}{2}\,\text{doz} \quad = & 0\cdot 16 \\
& \phantom{0}3 = \tfrac{1}{4}\,\text{doz} \quad = & \underline{0\cdot 08} \\
& \text{Cost of 57 eggs} \quad = & \underline{\underline{\pounds 1\cdot 52}}
\end{array}
$$

*Example 3:*
    If eggs are sold in a crate of 30 dozen boxes and the price is quoted at £9·00 per crate, find the cost of 10 eggs:

$$\text{cost of 1 dozen} \ = \frac{\pounds 9\cdot 00}{30} = 30\text{p per dozen}$$

$$\text{cost of 10 eggs} \ = \frac{5}{6} \times \frac{30}{1} = 25\text{p}$$
$(\tfrac{5}{6}\text{ of a dozen})$

      (1 egg costs 2·5p)

Prices of milk, vinegar, ice cream and other commodities will be quoted by the litre:

*Example 4:*
    Find the cost of 4·5 litres of milk at 40p per litre:

$$
\begin{array}{ll}
40\times & \text{(multiply as if by a whole number then move} \\
\underline{4\cdot 5} & \text{decimal point 1 place to left in answer)} \\
\underline{\underline{180}} &
\end{array}
$$

$=\pounds 1\cdot 80$

*Example 5:*
    Find the cost of 150 millilitres of double cream at £1·40 per litre:

$$
\begin{array}{ll}
& \qquad\pounds \\
100\,\text{ml} = & 0\cdot 14 \ (\tfrac{1}{10}\text{ of litre}) \\
\phantom{1}50\,\text{ml} = & \underline{0\cdot 07} \ (\tfrac{1}{2}\text{ above}) \\
& \underline{\underline{\pounds 0\cdot 21}}
\end{array}
$$

# Averages of weights

It is often necessary to have to calculate average weights for costing or estimating purposes.

If the average weight of the following is required:

| 5 bags weighing: | kg |
|---|---|
| 1 | 1·240 |
| 2 | 1·120 |
| 3 | 1·375 |
| 4 | 1·895 |
| 5 | 1·400 |
| | 5)7·030 |

Average weight per bag = 1·406 kg

# Mixtures and blends

Mixtures and blends are often used in catering, the commodities differing in price. Finding the cost of the mixture or blend is another form of averaging.

*Example 1:*

Find the average cost of a mixture of tea made up as follows:

|  | £ |
|---|---|
| 1   kg at 66p per kg = | 0·66 |
| 1·5  kg at 74p per kg = | 1·11 |
| 0·5  kg at 84p per kg = | 0·42 |
| 3·0  kg | £2·19 |

Average cost of 1 kg $= \dfrac{£2·19}{3} = 73p$

*Example 2:*

A mixed spice is made up from 5 ingredients. Find the cost of 30 g of the mixture if the following amounts are used:

| Ingredients | kg | | | £ |
|---|---|---|---|---|
| 1 | 0·5 | at 40p per kg | = | 0·200 |
| 2 | 0·15 | at 96p per 500 g | = | 0·288 |
| 3 | 0·5 | at 64p per kg | = | 0·320 |
| 4 | 0·25 | at £1·28 per kg | = | 0·320 |
| 5 | 0·375 | at 16p per 500 g | = | 0·120 |
| | 1·775 | | | £1·248 (say £1·25) |

Cost of 30 g $= \dfrac{0·03}{1·775} \times \dfrac{£1·25}{1} = 2·11p$

*Example 3 :*

If 3·5 kg of sultanas at £16·80 per 50 kg and 2·5 kg of currants at £14·56 per 50 kg are used to make a mixture, what is the cost of 1 kg of the mixture?

|  | Cost of 50 kg £ | Cost of 1 kg £ | Cost of qty used | £ |
|---|---|---|---|---|
| sultanas | 16·80 | ¯0·336 | 3·5 kg | 1·176 |
| currants | 14·56 | 0·2912 | 2·5 kg | 0·728 |
| mixture |  |  | 6·0 kg | 1·904 |

Cost of 1 kg = £1·904 ÷ 6 = £0·3173 or 32p (to nearest penny)

# Progress test questions

1. Calculate the cost of 1½ dozen capons weighing 2·375 kg each at 56p per kilo.

2. Calculate the following:
   4 fans of celery (12 heads to a fan) at 18p per head
   3 boxes of chicory (5 kg to a box) at 110p per kg
   Half bag of carrots (25 kg to a bag) at 18p per kg
   5 crates of leeks (10 kg to a crate) at 24p per kg
   8 trays of tomatoes (6 kg to a tray) at 56p per kg
   3 chips of gooseberries (6 kg to a chip) at 30p per kg
   1 case of grapefruit (60 to a case) at 8p each
   1 bushell of pears (20 kg to a bushell) at 26p per kg
   1 crate of eggs (360) to a crate) at 34p per dozen.

3. If lard is quoted at £6·70 per 50 kg, calculate the cost of 6·75 kg.

4. Eggs are quoted at £13·68 per crate of 360. If 45 are used in the kitchen, calculate the cost.

5. Calculate the cost of 11·5 litres of milk at 80p per 5 litres.

6. A blend of tea is made up of:
   0·5 kg at 76p per kg
   1·5 kg at 72p per kg
   1·375 kg at 68p per kg.
   Calculate the cost of ½ kg of the blend.

7. Using the approximate equivalent table convert the following recipe into metric measures:

*Fricassée of chicken* (8 portions)
2 × 2½ lb chickens
3 oz butter
3 oz flour
2 teaspoons chopped parsley
4 level teaspoons salt
½ level teaspoon ground white pepper
2 pints chicken stock
¼ pint cream
2 yolks of egg
Small bouquet garni
*Garnish* 2 oz butter
       4 oz bread

8. Calculate the cost of the following (using the actual equivalent table)
   27 lb of dessert apples at 33p per kg
   2 lb 6 oz luncheon meat at £1·20 per kg
   ¾ gallon milk at 17p per litre.

*Answers:* (1) £23·94, (2) £91·87, (3) £0·9045 (90½p), (4) £1·71, (5) £1·84, (6) £0·3548 (35½p), (8) £5·9137 (£5·91½).

CHAPTER 2

# The Basic Elements of Cost

## Basic elements of cost

The hotelier and caterer are selling food and service, and their selling prices must cover:

*1. Food cost.* This is the material used in the production of meals to be sold.

*2. Labour cost.* This cost is calculated from the weekly payroll plus any payments made for casual labour. It includes the gross pay, plus the employer's National Insurance contributions. This is the cost of employing staff, and added to this must be the cost of supplying meals and accommodation to the staff.

*3. Overheads.* These are the expenses of running the establishment such as rent, rates, gas, electricity, fuel, printing, stationery, advertising, cleaning and laundry, cleaning materials, repairs and renewals, telephone, insurances, legal fees, sundry expenses, depreciation and any other expenses typical of the catering industry.

*4. Net profit.* This is the reward for capital invested in the business.

The selling prices of the establishment have to be fixed to cover the food cost, labour cost, overheads and yield a reasonable net profit. These are called the *basic elements of cost* and are calculated as a percentage of the selling price, which always represents 100%.

Fig. 2.1   Elements of cost, gross and net profit

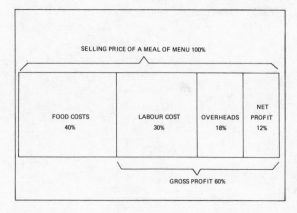

SELLING PRICE OF A MEAL OF MENU 100%

| FOOD COSTS 40% | LABOUR COST 30% | OVERHEADS 18% | NET PROFIT 12% |

GROSS PROFIT 60%

# Formulae

$$\frac{\text{Selling price}}{100\%} - \frac{\text{Food cost}}{40\%} = \frac{\text{Gross profit}}{60\%}$$

$$\frac{\text{Gross profit}}{60\%} - \frac{\text{Labour} + \text{Overheads}}{(30\% + 18\%)} = \frac{\text{Net profit}}{12\%}$$

$$\frac{\text{Selling price}}{100\%} - \frac{(\text{Food cost} + \text{Labour} + \text{Overheads})}{(40\% + 30\% + 18\%)} = \frac{\text{Net profit}}{12\%}$$

*To simplify:*
Every £1 taken in Fig. 2.1 for sales is thus divided:

| | |
|---|---|
| 40p | for Food |
| 30p | for Labour |
| 18p | for Overheads |
| 12p | for Net profit |
| £1·00 | Sales |

*Example 1:*
For the month of May the sales for the Merton Restaurant were
£4,200, Food cost £1,554, Labour cost £1,386, Overheads £714:

*Food cost:* $\dfrac{1,554}{4,200} \times 100 = 37\%$

*Labour cost:* $\dfrac{1,386}{4,200} \times 100 = 33\%$

*Overheads:* $\dfrac{714}{4,200} \times 100 = 17\%$

*Net profit* (Sales − Food cost + Labour + Overheads):

$$\frac{546}{4,200} \times 100 = 13\%$$

### Merton Restaurant

#### Cost and Profit Statement for May 19 . .

| | £ | % of Sales |
|---|---|---|
| Food cost | 1,554·00 | 37 |
| Labour cost | 1,386·00 | 33 |
| Overheads | 714·00 | 17 |
| Net profit | 546·00 | 13 |
| Sales | £4,200·00 | 100% |

# Different types of establishment

The percentages of the basic elements of cost can vary according to the type of establishment and the service it provides.

In an establishment with luxurious furnishings and silver service at table, providing a high standard of cuisine and service, the labour and overheads costs will be much higher than for the average establishment with average furnishings and providing simple meals or perhaps even self-service.

The caterer himself decides what gross profit he requires to cover his labour and overheads and to give him a reasonable net profit, and he fixes his selling prices accordingly. Alternatively, the selling prices may, to a degree, be determined for the caterer by what his customers are prepared to pay, or the average selling prices of his immediate competitors.

*Example 2:*

If, after consideration of his competitors' prices, a caterer fixes the selling price of his table d'hôte dinner menu at £2·50 per cover exclusive of Value Added Tax, and it is necessary for him to make a minimum 70% gross profit in order to cover his labour costs, overheads and provide a reasonable net profit, then his food cost must not exceed 30%:

Selling price − Gross profit = Food cost
100%          70%          30%

If the menu is £2·50 exclusive of Value Added Tax, the food cost must be no more than:

$$\frac{30}{200} \times £2\cdot50 = 75\text{p per cover}$$

This means the caterer must plan his menu with a maximum food cost of 75p per cover, and the meal must be of such quality and variety that his customer will be prepared to pay £2·50 for it—which proves the necessity for skilful menu planning.

# Turnover and profit margins

By comparing two restaurants we can clearly see how the basic elements of cost can vary according to the type of establishment and the standard of food and service provided, even though the turnover figures are the same.

*Example 3:*

| | Apex Restaurant June 19.. | | Park Restaurant June 19.. | |
|---|---|---|---|---|
| | £ | % | £ | % |
| Food cost | 2,100 | 42 | 1,750 | 35 |
| Labour cost | 1,400 | 28 | 1,600 | 32 |
| Overheads | 1,000 | 20 | 1,150 | 23 |
| Net profit | 500 | 10 | 500 | 10 |
| Sales | £5,000 | 100 | £5,000 | 100 |
| Gross profit | £2,900 | 58% | £3,250 | 65% |

Both restaurants have achieved the same net profit, but it will be observed that the Park Restaurant is operating on a higher gross profit margin. The labour and overheads costs are higher which indicates that this restaurant is of a more luxurious type than the Apex Restaurant, even though the food cost percentage is lower.

# Materials (food cost)

Having carefully calculated the cost of menus or individual dishes to be sold, constant surveillance must be kept on the cost of food sold percentage. Usually monthly food costs and gross profit statements are prepared to see how the actual operations compare with the expectations. The calendar month or accounting period of four or five weeks is used.

The calculation of the food cost for the month is determined by valuing the stock that was on hand at the beginning of the month, to which is added the purchases less any returns made during the month; from this total the value of the stock at the end of the month will be subtracted; the result is the cost of food sold during the month.

*Example 4:*

Food cost for July 19 . .

| | £ | £ |
|---|---|---|
| Stock 1 July | | 125 |
| *Add* Purchases | 700 | |
| *Less* Returns | 25 | 675 |
| | | 800 |
| *Less* Stock 31 July | | 100 |
| Cost of food sold | | £700 |

If the sales (turnover) for the month are £2,000:

$$\text{Sales} \quad - \quad \text{Food cost} = \text{Gross profit} \quad (\text{Kitchen profit})$$
$$£2,000 \qquad £700 \qquad £1,300$$

Therefore the gross profit percentage is:

$$\frac{\text{Gross profit}}{\text{Sales}} = \frac{1,300}{2,000} \times 100 = 65\%$$

If the food cost percentage shows unusual variances, this could be due to any of the following reasons, and immediate investigation and corrective action should be taken:

1. Excessive wastage in the kitchen
2. Pilfering
3. Carelessness in portion control
4. Increases in the purchase price of commodities
5. Bad purchasing
6. Suppliers not keeping to specifications
7. Overcharging or clerical errors in invoices
8. Change in sales mix (e.g. increase in salads—fall in sale of hot meals due to changing seasons)

# Staff meals

The hotelier and caterer usually provide meals for their staff, and this is an important cost that must be taken into consideration when calculating the percentage cost of food sold. The cost of staff meals is in fact part of the cost of employing labour and therefore *must be deducted from the cost of food consumed and transferred to the labour cost* in order to arrive at an accurate percentage.

*Example 5:*

*Food cost for July 19 . .*

|  | £ | £ |
|---|---|---|
| Stock 1 July |  | 125 |
| *Add* Purchases | 700 |  |
| *Less* Returns | 25 |  |
|  |  | 675 |
|  |  | 800 |
| *Less* Stock 31 July |  | 100 |
| Cost of food consumed |  | 700 |
| *Less* Staff meals |  | 66 |
| Cost of food sold |  | £634 |

If the sales turnover for the month is £2,000:

Sales   − Food cost = Gross profit (Kitchen profit)
£2,000      £634      £1,366

Therefore the *gross profit percentage* is:

$$\frac{\text{Gross profit}}{\text{Sales}} = \frac{1,366}{2,000} \times 100 = 68\cdot3\%$$

Compare this example with Example 4 and you can see how staff meals can affect the gross profit percentage.

## *Calculation of staff meals*

Most caterers calculate an average food cost per meal, and for full-time staff they allow breakfast, luncheon and dinner plus an amount for drinks. Therefore, if the food cost for breakfast is 15p, lunch 25p and dinner 35p, then the daily food cost for full-time staff would be 75p per day. Part-time and staff on split duties have their meals calculated in accordance with what meals they have whilst on duty.

*Example 6:*

Daily summary

Staff meals allowances

*15 June 19 . .*

|  |  | No. of persons | Cost | £ |
|---|---|---|---|---|
| Meals | Full-time | 15 | @ 75p | 11·25 |
|  | Part-time | 6 | @ 40p | 2·40 |
| Drinks | Full-time | 15 | @ 20p | 3·00 |
|  | Part-time | 6 | @ 10p | 0·60 |
| Reception staff | Full-time | 5 | @ 45p | 2·25 |
|  | Part-time | 3 | @ 35p | 1·05 |
| Maintenance | Full-time | 2 | @ 75p | 1·50 |
|  | Part-time | 2 | @ 40p | 0·80 |
| Gardeners/Florists | Full-time | 1 | @ 45p | 0·45 |
|  | Part-time | 1 | @ 25p | 0·25 |
| Chance |  | 1 | @ 40p | 0·40 |
|  |  |  |  | £23·95 |

# Monthly comparative percentage statements

These are prepared in order that the management can make comparisons and note variances in percentages.

*Example 7:*

*Monthly comparative percentage statement*

|  | April | % of Sales | May | % of Sales | June | % of Sales |
|---|---|---|---|---|---|---|
| Food cost | £1,600 | 40 | £1,615 | 38 | £1,645 | 35 |
| Labour cost | 1,120 | 28 | 1,190 | 28 | 1,363 | 29 |
| Overheads | 880 | 22 | 850 | 20 | 846 | 18 |
| Net profit | 400 | 10 | 595 | 14 | 846 | 18 |
| Sales | £4,000 | 100% | £4,250 | 100% | £4,700 | 100% |
| | | | | | | |
| Gross profit | £2,400 | 60% | £2,635 | 62% | £3,055 | 65% |

As can be seen from the foregoing statement:

1. The food cost percentage has decreased steadily; this could be due to the change of season, which could result in falling sales of hot meals and an increase in sales of salads. It could also indicate less wastage and more efficiency in the kitchen

2. The labour cost percentage remains fairly constant

3. The overheads percentage has steadily decreased, which reflects the automatic reduction of heat and light as power consumption decreases in summer

# Catering returns

Most hoteliers and caterers also prepare monthly catering returns showing details of the elements of costs expressed as percentages of sales. Caterers of the future have to think carefully in terms of these percentages and use them to promote cost-consciousness in the staff. Constant comparisons will provide the management with control information and promote profit efficiency.

*Example 8:*

**Apex Restaurant**

*Profit and loss percentage statement for June 19 . .*

| | £ | £ | £ | % of Sales |
|---|---|---|---|---|
| *Food cost* | | | | |
| Opening stock | | 75 | | |
| *Add* Purchases | 2,075 | | | |
| *Less* Returns | 25 | | | |
| | | 2,050 | | |
| | | 2,125 | | |
| *Less* Closing stock | | 70 | | |
| | | 2,055 | | |
| *Less* Staff meals | | 60 | | |
| | | | 1,995 | 38 |
| *Labour cost* | | | | |
| Kitchen | | 1,120 | | |
| Restaurant | | 710 | | |
| *Add* Staff meals | | 60 | | |
| | | | 1,890 | 36 |
| *Overheads* | | | | |
| Rent and rates | | 140 | | |
| Fuel and light | | 180 | | |
| Cleaning and laundry | | 85 | | |
| Repairs and renewals | | 75 | | |
| Printing and stationery | | 45 | | |
| Postage | | 60 | | |
| Telephone | | 45 | | |
| Sundry expenses | | 50 | | |
| Depreciation | | 160 | | |
| | | | 840 | 16 |
| *Net profit* | | | 525 | 10 |
| Sales | | | £5,250 | 100% |
| | | | | |
| Sales | | | £5,250 | 100% |
| *Less* Food cost | | | 1,995 | 38% |
| Gross profit (Kitchen profit) | | | £3,255 | 62% |

# Progress test questions

1. Explain what is meant by the basic elements of cost.
2. Prepare cost and profit statements from the following information:

   (a) Sales for June £3,750, Overheads £675, Labour cost £1,125, Food cost £1,425

(b) Food cost £2,496, Labour cost £1,792, Overheads £1,152, Sales for May £6,400

3. (a) From the following information prepare a comparative percentage statement for the Seabee Restaurant, calculate the gross profit and net profit and express each element of cost as a percentage of sales.

|  | November 19.. £ | December 19.. £ |
|---|---|---|
| Sales | 4,600 | 5,300 |
| Food cost | 1,610 | 2,014 |
| Labour | 1,288 | 1,590 |
| Overheads | 1,012 | 1,166 |

(b) Study your prepared statement and give what you think are the reasons for the variances of the percentages of the basic elements of cost.

4. (a) If a hotel has to fix the selling price of its table d'hôte menu at £2·20 per cover, exclusive of Value Added Tax, and a gross profit margin of 65% has to be obtained, calculate the maximum food cost that can be allowed for the menu.

(b) The Belle View Hotel serves a table d'hôte menu at £1·75 per cover, exclusive of Value Added Tax; calculate the food cost of the menu if the management requires a 60% gross profit margin.

5. Calculate the cost of food consumed from the following:

(a) Stock 1 August          £72
    Stock 31 August         £88
    Purchases for the month of August   £980
    Purchases returns       £24

(b) Purchases for the month of March   £720
    Stock 1 March           £45
    Purchases returns       £18
    Stock 31 March          £54

(c) Give reasons which could be the cause of the food cost percentage of a restaurant showing unusual variances.

6. (a) What is the correct method of dealing with staff meals from a costing point of view?

(b) The Obana Hotel employs ten full-time staff taking breakfast, lunch and dinner; five part-time staff who take breakfast and lunch; two reception staff who have lunch and dinner; one

maintenance man who takes dinner and breakfast, and one
gardener and one florist who take breakfast. The estimated food
cost of meals are: breakfast 15p, lunch 20p, dinner 30p; there is
also a drinks allowance of 15p for all full-time staff, and 10p for all
part-time staff. Prepare the daily staff meals summary sheet for
June 19 . .

7. Calculate the kitchen profit and net profit from the following
information:

(a) Sales £3,200, Cost of food consumed £1,410, Staff meals £66,
Labour cost £830, Overheads £544

(b) Food cost £2,554, Labour cost £1,866, Overheads £1,170, Staff
meals £84, Sales £6,500

and express each element as a percentage of sales.

8. From the records of the South Sea Restaurant the following figures
were extracted for the month of September. Prepare a costs and profits
statement, expressing each element of cost as a percentage of sales:

|  | £ |
|---|---|
| Stock 1 September | 125 |
| Stock 30 September | 110 |
| Purchases | 1,660 |
| Purchases returns | 25 |
| Staff meals | 120 |
| Wages | 1,240 |
| Rates | 120 |
| Heat and light | 140 |
| Repairs and maintenance | 110 |
| Telephone | 32 |
| Sundry expenses | 63 |
| Advertising | 25 |
| Cleaning materials | 65 |
| Depreciation | 210 |
| Sales | 4,250 |

9. The following figures were extracted from the records of the Mitre
Restaurant. Prepare a costs and profits percentage statement for the
month of April 19 . . and express each element as a percentage of sales.

|  | £ |
|---|---|
| Stock 1 April | 122 |
| Net purchases | 3,064 |
| Stock 30 April | 90 |
| Staff meals | 132 |

| | |
|---|---:|
| Restaurant wages | 1,320 |
| Kitchen wages | 1,036 |
| Gas | 180 |
| Electricity | 75 |
| Fuel | 110 |
| Advertising | 25 |
| Telephone | 32 |
| Cleaning materials | 30 |
| Sundry expenses | 70 |
| Depreciation | 300 |
| Renewals | 48 |
| Rates | 180 |
| Insurance | 45 |
| Rent | 324 |
| Printing and stationery | 25 |
| Sales | 7,600 |

# CHAPTER 3

# Calculation of Selling Prices

## Portion control

To ensure customer satisfaction the caterer will serve a fair portion of food for a fair price. To maintain profitability on all portions sold, the caterer will ensure that once the portion sizes to be served are established, then strict portion control will be implemented by both supervisors and staff.

The prices quoted in the following examples are based on 1976 prices. They are only used to illustrate a method or point and are not intended to indicate current prices.

## *Determination of portion sizes*

When determining the size of portions to be served the caterer will consider the following factors:

1. *The type of customer to be catered for.* The nature of a person's work can have an effect on his appetite and eating habits. If the restaurant caters in the main for manual workers, then the menu would usually be basic and the portion sizes larger than if it were catering for office workers, who would probably prefer more variety in the menu and smaller portion sizes.

2. *The type of establishment.* In a medium-standard restaurant providing a three of four-course table d'hôte meal at a reasonable price, the portion sizes would be average. A high class establishment with a comprehensive à la carte menu would attract customers who preferred variety in their food and the portion would also be of a medium size and in keeping with the type of food and price charged. In an exclusive restaurant where the emphasis is on high quality cuisine and service, the portion sizes must reflect the prices charged. For example, if a customer is prepared to pay about £4·50 for roast prime ribs of beef *au jus* with accompanying vegetables, he would be entitled to show dissatisfaction if presented with a 110–170 g portion of beef; a portion of at least 225–340 g would be more in keeping with the price.

3. *Customer spending power.* Many hotels and restaurants have to fix their prices according to the average spending power of their customers. The size of portion they can offer at a set price will depend on how

much the customer can afford to spend. For example, a restaurateur could possibly sell to his customers a 170 g fillet steak with accompaniments for £2·25, but if he offered a 280 g fillet steak for £3·50, he might have difficulty in selling it, because although the 280 g fillet steak is equally good value for money, the customer's spending power may be limited.

The following list is a guide to the average number of portions obtainable from various foods and the size of the average portion served in a medium-class restaurant, but it must be borne in mind that the actual portion sizes served will depend on the style of the establishment and the type of customer served.

| *Soups* | 1 litre | 3–5 portions |
|---|---|---|
| | 1 pint | 2–3 portions |
| *Fish* | | |
| Cod | | |
| Fresh haddock ⎫ | 120 g (¼ lb) | 1 portion |
| Salmon ⎭ | | |
| Herring, trout (whole) | 180–225 g (6–8 oz) | 1 portion |
| Mackerel, whiting (whole) | 225–280 g (8–10 oz) | 1 portion |
| Plaice | 560 g (1¼ lb) (4 fillets) | 2 portions |
| Whole plaice | 225–280 g (8–10 oz) | 1 portion |
| Cold salmon | 110–140 g (4–5 oz) | 1 portion |
| Slip sole | 170–225 g (6–8 oz) | 1 portion |
| Whole sole | 280–340 g (10–12 oz) | 1 portion |
| Sole for filleting | 560–680 g (1¼–1½ lb) | 1 portion |
| Turbot, brill (whole) | 3 kg (6·6 lb) | 10 portions (approx.) |
| Whitebait | 1 kg (2·2 lb) | 10 portions |
| *Poultry* | | |
| Baby chicken | 340–390 g (12–14 oz) | 1 portion |
| Double baby chicken | 560–680 g (1¼–1½ lb) | 2 portions |
| Small roasting chicken | 1–1·1 kg (2¼–2½ lb) | 4 portions |
| Medium roasting chicken | 1·1–2 kg (2½–4 lb) | 4–6 portions |
| Large roasting chicken | 2–3 kg (4½–6½ lb) | 6–10 portions |
| Large boiling chicken | 2·5–3·5 kg (5–8 lb) | 7–10 portions |
| Duckling | 1·5–2 kg (3¼–4½ lb) | 4 portions |
| Duck | 2–3 kg (4½–6½ lb) | 5–6 portions |
| Gosling | 3–3·5 kg (6½–7½ lb) | 7–9 portions |
| Goose | 3·5–7 kg (7½–15 lb) | 9–18 portions |
| Young turkey | 3–4·5 kg (6½–10 lb) | 14–16 portions |
| Hen/Cock turkey | 3·5–13·5 kg (7½–30 lb) | 16–60 portions |

| Meats | | | | |
|---|---|---|---|---|
| *Beef—* | Roast | 170–225 g (6–8 oz) | per portion | |
| | Boiled, braised | } 110–170 g (4–6 oz) | per portion | |
| | Stews, pies, puddings | | | |
| | Steaks | 110–225 g (4–8 oz) | per portion | |
| *Lamb—* | Roast | 110–170 g (4–6 oz) | per portion | |
| | Stewed | 170–225 g (6–8 oz) | per portion | |
| | Cutlets | 110 g (4 oz) | per portion | |
| | Chop | 110–170 g (4–6 oz) | per portion | |
| *Pork—* | Roast | 110–170 g (4–6 oz) | per portion | |
| | Chop | 170–225 g (6–8 oz) | per portion | |
| | Ham and cold meats | 55–85 g (2–3 oz) | per portion | |
| *Offal—* | Lamb, pig, ox liver | 120 g (4 oz) | per portion | |
| | Sweetbreads | 85–120 g (3–4 oz) | per portion | |
| | Kidneys | 2 | per portion | |
| | Ox Tongue | 170–240 g (6–8 oz) | per portion | |
| *Vegetables* | | 85–110 g (3–4 oz) | per portion | |
| *Sauces* | | 30–55 g (1–2 oz) | per portion | |

# Equipment

Having established the portion sizes to be served, the caterer must make sure that the correct equipment to implement portion control is available and that the use of it is demonstrated to the staff.

*Basic equipment for portion control is as follows:*
  Standard recipe charts
  Bar optics
  Butter pat machines
  Graded size scoops and ladles
  Measuring jugs
  Milk and tea dispensers
  Scales
  Slicing machines
  Standard-sized baking tins, coupes, cups, glasses, moulds, plates, soup bowls.

# Standard recipes

Calculations of selling prices are based on the cost of the dish or menu produced. The ingredients used and the number of portions produced from the recipe are the basis of the costing. Therefore most catering organisations, whether large or small, evolve what is known as their 'manual'. This is a file of successful standard recipes from which they plan their menus. The ingredients of these recipes are costed out and the number of portions expected from each recipe is fixed. As prices fluctuate the costings are amended accordingly. It is essential that the ingredients and quantities used in these standard recipes are strictly adhered to, and that the portions produced from them do not vary. Any variation from either recipe or number of portions produced will invalidate the costing and consequently the calculation of the selling price; this could result in a loss to the caterer.

*Example 1: Standard recipe*

   *Dish:* Scrambled egg with ham on toast
   *Yield:* 100 portions
      Allow 30 g ham per portion

| Quantity | Ingredients | Unit cost | Unit cost | Unit cost | Unit cost |
|---|---|---|---|---|---|
| 4 litres | White sauce | | | | |
| 200 | Eggs | | | | |
| 1 kg | Butter | | | | |
| 3 kg | Ham | | | | |
| 8 | Sandwich loaves | | | | |
| 60 g | Salt | | | | |
| 30 g | Pepper | | | | |
| | Total cost | | | | |
| | Cost per portion | | | | |
| | Menu price | | | | |
| | Gross profit % | | | | |

(The costing of standard recipes is dealt with in Chapter 4.)

# Staff instruction

It must not be assumed that staff know of the importance of portion control. It is the responsibility of chefs and supervisors to instruct their staff on the correct use of equipment, and explain why it is necessary to adhere to the standard recipes and serve the correct portion sizes. Portion charts should be displayed at convenient points in the kitchen as a constant reminder. Regular demonstrations should be given as to exactly what the set portion size looks like, e.g. a 120 gramme portion of chips or a 150 gramme portion of beef stew. This visual training will encourage all members of staff to use their eyes and be on the alert for variations in portion sizes.

# Regular checking

Food and beverage controllers should do regular spot checks on the food leaving the kitchen for quality, portion size and presentation. Portion sizes should be occasionally checked on the scales. The number of portions sold should be cross-checked against the number of portions expected to be produced from the commodities used by the kitchen.

# Pre-packed and individual portions

The individual portion control concept is being increasingly used by hotels, self-service restaurants, canteens, cafeterias, the school meals service, hospitals, take-away meal counters, airlines, ships and railways. Manufacturers are constantly extending their range of individual portions to meet the changing need of contemporary catering.

The extra cost of preparation of individual portions is reflected in the purchase price, but caterers often feel that the many advantages offset the increase in cost:

1. Convenience
2. Exact portion and cost control
3. No preparation required
4. Time and labour saved
5. No waste or mess
6. Hygienic
7. Meal trays can be prepared in advance of use
8. Consistent and attractive presentation of individual portions.

As well as pre-portioned meat and fish, other products are now being pre-packed in individual portions, for example:

Jams, marmalade and honey
Sauces and dressings
Dairy products, i.e. butter, cheese, milk, cream
Condiments, i.e. salt, pepper, mustard
Sugar

# Calculation of selling prices

When a caterer prepares a dish which costs 30p to make, and sells it for 75p, the difference between the cost and the selling price is called the *gross profit*, in this case 45p.

*Formula:*  Sales − Food cost = Gross profit
75p        30p            45p

This gross profit (or kitchen profit as it is called in catering) has to be sufficient to pay for all the expenses of running the business and leave a reasonable amount, called net profit, for the caterer. It is standard practice to express the gross profit (kitchen profit) and net profit as a percentage of sales or takings.

## Mark-up

The amount added to the cost price of an item to give the selling price is known as the 'mark-up'. This amount, which is in effect the gross profit, is usually expressed as a percentage mark-up on the cost price.

Cost price of dish 30p—selling price 75p

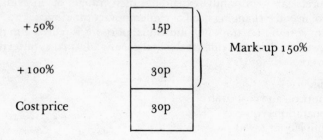

## Margin

This term is used when the gross profit is expressed as a percentage of the selling price. The selling price is always expressed as 100%.

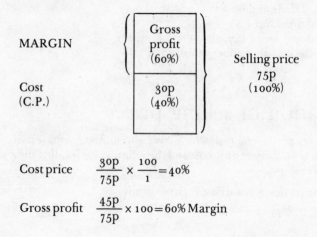

Cost price $\dfrac{30p}{75p} \times \dfrac{100}{1} = 40\%$

Gross profit $\dfrac{45p}{75p} \times 100 = 60\%$ Margin

From this example you can see that the caterer has to mark up 150% on cost in order to obtain a 60% gross profit margin. Note the mark-up necessary to obtain the following margins:

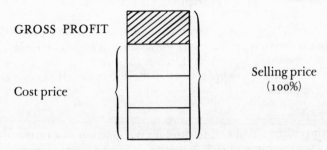

*Note:* If mark-up is 33⅓% (⅓ of cost price), margin is 25% (¼ of selling price).

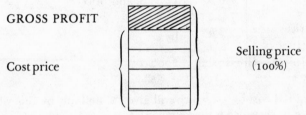

*Note:* If mark-up is 25% (¼ of cost price), margin is 20% (⅕ of selling price).

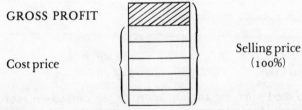

*Note:* If mark-up is 20% (⅕ of cost price), margin is 16⅔% (⅙ of selling price).

Caterers usually find it more useful to calculate the 'margin', that is, the rate of gross profit, in relation to the sales (turnover) figures. For example, if the selling prices have been fixed to give a certain gross profit margin then it is a simple matter to calculate what amount of the sales takings can be considered Gross Profit.

41

*Example 2:*

If sales (turnover) for the month are £6,000 and the caterer is working on a 60% gross profit margin, then

$$\frac{60}{100} \times \frac{£6,000}{1} = £3,600 \text{ gross profit (kitchen profit)}$$

When fixing selling prices, the caterer must determine what percentage gross profit will be required to cover the labour costs and overheads and provide a reasonable net profit. He can then cost out the dishes he proposes selling and 'mark up' the cost of the dish to yield the gross profit margin he requires.

*Example 3:*

The ingredients required to produce one portion of a certain dish cost 35p. The caterer needs to make a 65% gross profit margin.

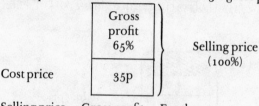

Selling price − Gross profit = Food cost
(100%)                   65%           35%

Divide food cost by 35, which will give 1%, multiply by 100, which will give 100%, which is the selling price:

$$\therefore \frac{C.P.}{35} \times 100 = \text{Selling price}$$

$$\therefore \frac{35}{35} \times 100 = £1 \cdot 00$$

# Supplement

This term is used when the amount added to the food cost is expressed as a percentage of the food cost:

*Example 4:*

| | |
|---|---|
| Selling price of a dish | £0·40 |
| Food cost | £0·25 |
| Supplement | £0·15 |

Supplement as a percentage of food cost $\quad \frac{0 \cdot 15}{0 \cdot 25} \times 100 = 60\%$

*Example 5:*

| | |
|---|---|
| Selling price of a dish | £0·75 |
| Food cost | £0·30 |
| Supplement | £0·45 |

Supplement expressed as a percentage of
food cost:

$$0·30 = 100\%$$
$$0·15 = 50\%$$
$$0·45 = 150\%$$

# Gross profit calculator

$$\text{Formula: Selling price} = \frac{\text{C.P.}}{45} \times \frac{100}{1} = \frac{\text{C.P.} \times 20}{9}$$

By using the formula, the following simple gross profit calculator can
be devised. (Note the sequence and memorise.)

| *Gross profit required* | *Formula* | *Mark-up* |
|---|---|---|
| 70% | $\dfrac{\text{C.P.} \times 20}{6}$ | $233\frac{1}{3}\% \, (\times 3·33)$ |
| 65% | $\dfrac{\text{C.P.} \times 20}{7}$ | $185\frac{5}{7}\% \, (\times 2·86)$ |
| 60% | $\dfrac{\text{C.P.} \times 20}{8}$ | $150\% \, (\times 2·5)$ |
| 55% | $\dfrac{\text{C.P.} \times 20}{9}$ | $122\frac{2}{9}\% \, (\times 2·22)$ |
| 50% | $\dfrac{\text{C.P.} \times 20}{10}$ | $100\% \, (\times 2)$ |
| 45% | $\dfrac{\text{C.P.} \times 20}{11}$ | $81\frac{9}{11}\% \, (\times 1·82)$ |

| Gross profit required | Formula | Mark-up |
|---|---|---|
| 40% | $\dfrac{\text{C.P.} \times 20}{12}$ | $66\frac{2}{3}\%\,(\times 1\cdot67)$ |
| 35% | $\dfrac{\text{C.P.} \times 20}{13}$ | $53\frac{11}{13}\%\,(\times 1\cdot54)$ |
| 30% | $\dfrac{\text{C.P.} \times 20}{14}$ | $42\frac{6}{7}\%\,(\times 1\cdot43)$ |
| 25% | $\dfrac{\text{C.P.} \times 20}{15}$ | $33\frac{1}{3}\%\,(\times 1\cdot33)$ |

To calculate odd percentages the principle involved is the same, e.g. gross profit required 52%:

Selling price (100%)

Cost price

$$\text{Formula}: \quad \frac{\text{C.P.}}{38} \times \frac{100}{1} = \text{Selling price}$$

By using the gross profit calculator, the caterer can calculate the selling price of a dish at different gross profit margins and select the price which the customer will be prepared to pay, and still enable him to make a reasonable net profit:

*Example 6:*

A dish costs 20p to produce.

Selling price at 70% gross profit margin:

$$\frac{\text{C.P.} \times 20}{6} = \frac{20 \times 20}{6} = \frac{200}{3} = 66\cdot6\text{p}\ (67\text{p})$$

Selling price at 65% gross profit margin:

$$\frac{\text{C.P.} \times 20}{7} = \frac{20 \times 20}{7} = \frac{400}{7} = 57\cdot1\text{p}\ (58\text{p})$$

Selling price at 55% gross profit margin:

$$\frac{\text{C.P.} \times 20}{9} = \frac{20 \times 20}{9} = \frac{400}{9} = 44\cdot4\text{p}\ (45\text{p})$$

## Profit margins on various dishes

Although the caterer may aim for a 60% gross profit margin on sales, it will not follow that every dish will be marked up to yield a 60% gross profit margin. The ingredients of certain fish and entrée dishes could be very expensive, and therefore it may be necessary to accept a lower profit margin on these dishes in order to sell them at a realistic price; conversely, it may be possible to achieve a much higher profit margin on certain soups, sweets and vegetables and still sell them at a reasonable price acceptable to the customer. If all dishes are costed it should be possible to compile the menu on the principle of 'what you lose on the swings you gain on the roundabouts', and achieve the overall gross profit margin required by the management.

# Pricing policy

The pricing policy of an establishment is a management decision and several factors have to be taken into consideration.

(a)  If, for example, a 60% gross profit margin on the previous year's sales (turnover) was necessary to cover labour and overhead costs and give a reasonable net profit, that percentage must be the minimum to aim for when deciding on future prices.
(b)  A knowledge of what customers are prepared to pay will be a guide to within what limits prices can be fixed.
(c)  A study of competitors' prices could also dictate in what range the prices have to be fixed in order to attract customers.

The management must decide exactly what factors are relevant to their particular establishment. If prices are controlled by their customers' spending power and their competitors' prices, then the approach to a pricing policy would be different from that of an establishment which sets out to attract customers of above-average spending power by offering a very high standard of cuisine and service.

*Example 7:*
> The restaurant of the Jamesville Hotel caters for customers whose average spending power has been calculated to be between £1·75 and £2·50 per head. The charge for a table d'hôte three-course lunch at other hotels in the area is from £1·25 to £2·50. The hotel requires at least a 62% gross profit margin to cover its labour costs and overheads and give a reasonable net profit.
> If the charge for a table d'hôte three-course lunch were fixed at £2·25 to keep in line with their customers' spending-power and competitors' prices, then to yield at least 62% gross profit the food cost for the menus offered must not exceed:

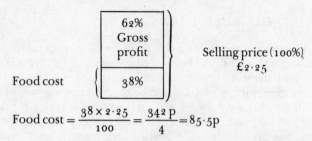

Food cost $= \dfrac{38 \times 2 \cdot 25}{100} = \dfrac{342\,\text{p}}{4} = 85 \cdot 5\text{p}$

The menus planned therefore must have a food cost of not more than $85\frac{1}{2}$p if the management are to make their necessary 62% gross profit margin.

*Example 8:*

The Excelsior Club caters for a very high-class clientèle who in the main choose their meals from the à la carte menu. The standard of the establishment requires that a gross profit of at least 68% is necessary to cover the high labour and overheads cost and yield a reasonable net profit. Therefore each dish on the à la carte menu is costed individually and marked up to yield at least a 68% margin:

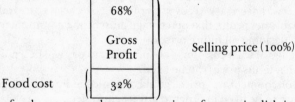

If the food cost to produce one portion of a certain dish is 48p, then in order to get a 68% gross profit margin it would have to go on the menu at a minimum selling price of:

*Formula:* $\dfrac{\text{C.P.} \times 100}{32} = \dfrac{0 \cdot 48 \times 100}{32} = £1 \cdot 50$ per portion

When deciding on their pricing policy, the management must always consider whether it is better to take a higher gross profit margin from a half-full restaurant or accept a lower profit margin from a full restaurant.

*Example 9:*

The turnover of the Mermaid Restaurant for a month was £2,000, working on a 60% gross profit margin:

$\therefore$ Gross profit $= \dfrac{60}{100} \times £2,000 = £1,200$

At this turnover the restaurant has not been functioning to its full capacity. The management feel that a gross profit of 55% would still be sufficient to cover the costs, although the net profit percentage would be lower. By lowering the selling prices the restaurant would possibly attract more customers and it is estimated that the turnover could be increased by £500 per month. The result would be:

$$\text{Gross profit} = \frac{55}{100} \times £2,500 = £1,375$$

By comparison 55% of £2,500 = £1,375
60% of £2,000 = £1,200

difference $\overline{\underline{£175}}$

*Conclusion:* If the other costs remain constant it is better to accept a lower gross profit margin from a high turnover (a full restaurant) than a high profit margin from a lower turnover (half-full restaurant).

# Progress test questions

1. Explain what factors the management must take into consideration when determining the portion sizes to be served in their establishment.

2. List at least ten items of equipment which will assist in portion control.

3. Explain the meaning of the following terms:
   (a) Mark-up
   (b) Margin
   (c) Supplement.

4. Calculate the following:

| Food cost of a dish | Gross profit margin required | Selling price |
|---|---|---|
| 20p | 60% | |
| 25p | 55% | |
| 36p | 65% | |
| 38p | 58% | |
| 42p | 70% | |
| 39p | 72% | |
| 42p | 65% | |
| 27p | 68% | |
| 48p | 45% | |
| 52p | 52% | |

5. Complete the following table:

| Selling price of menu | Gross profit margin required | Maximum food cost |
|---|---|---|
| £1·50 | 60% | |
| £0·95 | 55% | |
| £3·75 | 72% | |
| £2·25 | 65% | |
| £1·75 | 62% | |

6. Calculate the following:

| Food cost of a dish | Selling price | Supplement added, expressed as a % of food cost (to 1 decimal place) |
|---|---|---|
| £0·36 | £0·54 | |
| £0·60 | £1·05 | |
| £0·40 | £0·75 | |
| £0·38 | £0·95 | |
| £0·68 | £1·60 | |

7. When deciding on a pricing policy, what factors would need to be considered by the management of a new establishment?

8. Discuss the following statement: 'It is better to aim for a high gross profit margin from a two-thirds full restaurant than accept a lower gross profit margin from a full restaurant.'

9. As a supervisor, what steps would you take to ensure implementation of strict portion control in your kitchen?

10. List some of the advantages of pre-packed individual portions.

# CHAPTER 4

# Unit and Multiple Costing

## The recipe manual

The efficient and cost-conscious caterer will compile a recipe manual of stocks, sauces and all finished dishes that are suitable for the type of menu to be offered by the establishment: if the restaurant specialises, then the manual will consist of the recipes of the specialist-type dishes offered.

The object of compiling a recipe manual is to provide a measure of the standards to be maintained by the food-producing departments and to assist the chefs and management in effective day-to-day cost and portion control. It should be reviewed constantly and new recipes added on a regular basis so that there is always an up-to-date, comprehensive selection of dishes from which the menus can be planned.

For practical purposes the manual should be divided into sections, and the recipes based on a convenient portion yield suitable for the size of the catering operation; for example, in large organisations the recipes are worked out to a yield of 100 portions, while in small establishments the recipes are based on a 4, 6, 8, 10, 12, 20 or 24 portion yield per recipe.

A typical layout for the manual might be:

| | | |
|---|---|---|
| *Section* | 1 | Stocks—Sauces—Essences—Glazes—Thickenings |
| *Section* | 2 | Hors d'œuvre |
| *Section* | 3 | Soups |
| *Section* | 4 | Egg dishes |
| *Section* | 5 | Farinaceous dishes |
| *Section* | 6 | Fish dishes: |
| | | (a) Fried |
| | | (b) Grilled |
| | | (c) Meunière |
| | | (d) Poached |
| | | (e) Miscellaneous |
| *Section* | 7 | Entrées: |
| | | (a) Beef |
| | | (b) Lamb |
| | | (c) Pork |
| | | (d) Veal |
| | | (e) Bacon |
| | | (f) Grills |

(g) Poultry and game
(h) Miscellaneous

| Section | 8 | Potatoes |
| Section | 9 | Vegetables |
| Section | 10 | Salads |
| Section | 11 | Savouries |
| Section | 12 | Pastry |
| Section | 13 | Hot and cold sweets |
| Section | 14 | Miscellaneous dishes |

As the manual is specifically for the use of, and has to be adhered to, by the food-producing departments, it should be clearly indexed. Each recipe should show:

(a) The section number;
(b) The recipe number;
(c) The list of ingredients with the quantities to be used;
(d) The portion yield from each recipe;
(e) Any special instructions on method of preparation or service.

*Example 1:*
Section 1
Recipe No. 3                                                    Basic White Stock
Yield—40 pints

| Quantity | Ingredients | Approximate metric equivalent |
| --- | --- | --- |
| 20 lb | Beef bones | 9 kg |
| 2 lb | Onions | 800 g |
| 2 lb | Carrots | 800 g |
| 1 lb | Leeks | 400 g |
| 4 oz | Parsley stalk | 125 g |
| 1 head | Celery | 1 head |
| 6 oz | Salt | 160 g |
| 1 oz | Pepper | 30 g |
| 2 | Bay leaves | 2 |

*Example 2:*
Section 1
Recipe No. 12                                                   Mornay Sauce
Yield—10 pints                                          100 × 2 oz (50 g) portions

| Quantity | Ingredients | Approximate metric equivalent |
| --- | --- | --- |
| 1 lb | Cheddar cheese | 560 g |
| 9 pints | Basic white sauce (Section 1, Recipe 3) | 5 litres |

*Example 3 :*

Section 7
Recipe No. 52            Roast Chicken à l'Anglaise
Yield            100 × ¼ Chicken portions

| Quantity | Ingredients | *Approximate metric equivalent* |
|---|---|---|
| 25 × 2½ lb | Roasting chickens | 25 × 1·35 kg |
| 6½ lb | Streaky bacon | 3 kg |
| 3 lb | Game chips (Section 9, Recipe 14) | 1·6 kg |
| 10 pints | Bread sauce (Section 1, Recipe 23) | 5·7 litres |
| 1½ lb | White fat | 840 g |
| 3 lb | Watercress | 1·7 kg |
| 1 oz | Pepper | 30 g |
| 6 pints | Roast gravy (Section 1, Recipe 1) | 3·5 litres |

To be served with garnish of one rasher streaky bacon, 1 portion bread sauce, watercress, gravy and game chips

# Unit costing

Before any selling prices can be fixed it is necessary to prepare a unit costing card for every dish in the recipe manual. The cost of one unit or portion is ascertained by dividing the total cost of the recipe by the number of portions yielded. The cost of one portion is then marked-up to the given percentage gross profit margin required by the caterer to enable him to cover his labour costs and overhead cost and yield a reasonable net profit. It must be remembered, however, that the calculation indicates the *minimum* price for which the dish can be sold in order to achieve a given percentage gross profit, but it does not indicate the *maximum* selling price that can be fixed; that will depend on other factors, and ultimately on what the customer is prepared to pay.

## *Preparation of a unit costing card*

1. The date of the costing, and of any subsequent revisions to the costing, must be shown.
2. From the standard recipe the ingredients and quantities to be used should be listed.
3. The unit price of ingredients used are obtainable from suppliers' price lists or invoices of commodities supplied. As prices can fluctuate daily it is customary for caterers to apply a standard system of pricing, which means using an average standard price of a commodity over a period

of time. A watchful eye must be kept on the prices of commodities, for if they rise above the average price used in costings, then the costings must be revised and amended.

4. The number of portions to be yielded from the recipe must be indicated.

5. The size of the portion to be served must be specified, as any variances from this will invalidate the costing.

6. An estimated cost of £0·01 should be allowed for any seasoning used in the recipe.

7. All stocks and sauces should be costed accurately and this costing used when these stocks or sauces are used in preparation of or as an accompaniment to other dishes.

8. The ingredients used should be costed accurately to at least 4 decimal places, e.g. £0·0375.

9. When the cost of one portion is ascertained, it is advisable to mark up to the nearest whole penny above; for example, if one portion of a dish costs £0·1575 this would be marked up to £0·16 per portion and this figure would be the basis of calculating the selling price. This is considered advisable in basic costing, as caterers are dealing with perishable commodities and a margin should be allowed for any wastage.

### Unit Cost Card

Section 7                                              Date: . . . . . . . . . . . . . . .

Recipe No. 52

Dish: Roast Chicken and garnish

Yield: 100 × ¼ chicken portions

| Quantity | Ingredients | Unit cost | Total |
|---|---|---|---|
| | | | £ |
| 25 × 1·35 kg | Roasting chickens | 60p per kg | 20·25 |
| 3 kg | Streaky bacon | 55p per kg | 1·65 |
| 1·6 kg | Game chips | 20p per kg | 0·32 |
| 5·7 litres | Bread sauce | 30p per litre | 1·71 |
| 840 g | White fat | 48p per kg | 0·41 |
| 1·7 kg | Watercress | 40p per kg | 0·68 |
| 30 g | Pepper | | 0·01 |
| 3·5 litres | Roast gravy | 16p per litre | 0·56 |
| | | | £25·59 |

Cost of one portion: 0·2559 (26p)

| Date | Minimum Menu Price @ Gross Profit | % | |
|---|---|---|---|
| | | 65% | £0·7438 (75p) |
| | | 60% | £0·65 |
| | | 55% | £0·5777 (58p) |

# Menu costing

From the dishes in the recipe manual the caterer will compile his menus. The composition of the menu requires skill, comprehensive knowledge and the consideration of a number of factors, not the least being the cost factor.

## Service charge and VAT inclusive and exclusive

Certain establishments quote their menu prices exclusive of a service charge and/or VAT, which means they are added to the cost of the meal after the bill is totalled. If, however, the menu charges are quoted inclusive of a service charge and VAT, this means that an allowance for these extra costs must be included by management in working out minimum charges to yield the required gross profit margin. If menu charges are quoted inclusive of a 10% service charge and 8% VAT, the cost of a hypothetical dish priced at £1 would have to be increased as follows:

|                              | £       |
|------------------------------|---------|
|                              | £       |
| Cost without service or VAT  | 1·00    |
| 10% service charge           | 0·10    |
|                              | 1·10    |
| +8% VAT                      | 0·088   |
| Cost (to nearest 1p)         | £1·19   |

The minimum menu prices on the unit cost card shown above would have to be increased by about 19%:

| Gross profit | Service and tax not included | Service and tax included |
|--------------|------------------------------|--------------------------|
| 65%          | £0·7438 (75p)                | £0·8835 (90p)            |
| 60%          | 0·65                         | 0·7722 (78p)             |
| 55%          | 0·5777 (58p)                 | 0·6863 (70p)             |

## À la carte menus

The fixing of selling prices on the à la carte menu is relatively simple, as each dish is individually priced. The cost of one portion of every dish offered on the menu is obtained from the unit cost card, and the minimum menu price at a given gross profit margin is noted. After taking account of price fluctuation due to market trends and seasonal variations, and the customer spending power of the establishment, the selling price is then fixed for every dish.

*Example 4:*

À la carte menu
of a 4 star establishment
(all prices are inclusive of service charge and Value Added Tax)

#### Soups
Vichyssoise (hot or cold) 55p
Beef consommé Madrilène (hot or cold) 45p
Minestrone 55p
Cream of chicken 50p

#### Hors d'œuvre
Assorted Hors d'œuvre £1·50
Avocado Vinaigrette £1·05
Grapefruit cocktail 70p
Honeydew melon 85p

Smoked salmon £2·00
Smoked trout £1·25
Mortadella and
   salami sausages 90p

Chef's pâté £1·00
Prawn cocktail £1·20
Lobster cocktail £2·00

#### Egg Dishes
Omelettes £1·10
  Marie-Louise
  Spanish
  Asparagus
  Américaine
  Mushroom
  Cheese
Poached eggs princesse £1·00

#### Pasta
Spaghetti bolognaise 95p
Spaghetti napolitaine 95p
Spaghetti au beurre 90p

#### Fish
Dover sole: grilled or meunière £3·20
Fillet of sole: fried, goujons, caprice £3·30
Scampi: fried, meunière, provençale £2·80
Trout: grilled, amandine, grenobloise £1·90
Halibut: grilled or poached with Hollandaise sauce £2·35

#### Entrées
Médaillon de bœuf bourguignone £3·00
Entrecôte sauté Duroc £3·15
Escalope of veal Romarin £3·30
Supreme of chicken Rossini £2·25
Lamb chop tyrolienne £2·65
Calves Liver with bacon and onions £2·00

*Grills*
Mixed grill £2·75
Kidneys and bacon £1·95
Lamb cutlets £2·25
Fillet steak vert pré £3·25
Sirloin steak garni £3·00
Grilled gammon £2·00

*Cold Buffet*
Chicken £2·00
Veal and ham pie £2·00
Tongue £1·95
York ham £2·00
Rib of beef £2·15

*Salads*
Mixed, Green, Tomato, Niçoise, Potato 60p

*Vegetables*
French fried, croquette, sauté, boiled and creamed potatoes 35p
Selection of vegetables 50p

*Sweets*
Crème Caramel 50p    Pear Belle Hélène 65p    Assorted ice
creams 50p  Pineapple and Kirsch £1·00    Orange salad and
Kirsch 85p    Coupe Montmorency 65p    Fresh fruit salad 75p

*Cheeses*
Assorted with celery 60p          *Coffee* 25p

---

If this particular restaurant finds it necessary to make a gross profit margin of 65%, then the food cost of the above items would have to represent no more than 35% of the selling price:

*Example 5:*

   Lobster Cocktail    £2·00

   Food cost of one portion $\dfrac{35}{100} \times \dfrac{£2\cdot00}{1} = 70\text{p}$

*Example 6:*

   Minestrone Soup    £0·55

   Food cost of one portion $\dfrac{35}{100} \times \dfrac{55}{1} = \dfrac{77}{4} = 19\cdot25\text{p}$

*Example 7:*

Fillet Steak vert pré   £3·25

Food cost of one portion $\dfrac{35}{100} \times \dfrac{£3·25}{1} = \dfrac{455}{4} = £1·14$ to nearest penny

# À la carte breakfast menu

Many establishments offer an à la carte breakfast menu, from which the customer may select his breakfast according to his taste. An average serving of one continental breakfast is costed on a multiple cost sheet and the total cost is used as the basis for the calculation of the menu price. Other items offered on the menu are costed on a unit cost card and the menu price fixed individually.

Other methods of costing and charging guests are shown in the section on table d'hôte costing (below).

*Example 8:*

*Continental breakfast*   £1·00
Chilled fruit juices—Grapefruit, Orange, Pineapple
Croissants—Rolls—Toast
Butter—Jams—Marmalade
Tea—Coffee

*À la carte*

| | | |
|---|---|---|
| Cereals—All Bran, Cornflakes, Shredded Wheat, Porridge | | 25p |
| Stewed Prunes, figs, apples | | 30p |

| *Eggs* | | *Fish* | |
|---|---|---|---|
| Boiled—Poached | £0·60 | Poached haddock in cream | £1·00 |
| Scrambled | £0·85 | Kippers | |
| Omelettes to choice | £0·90 | Fried fillets of plaice } | £1·30 |
| Fried egg and bacon | £1·00 | | |

| *Grills* | | | |
|---|---|---|---|
| Sausages | £0·35 | Pancakes, waffles, griddle cakes | |
| Kidneys and bacon | £1·40 | with maple syrup | £0·40 |
| Tomatoes and mushrooms | £0·40 | | |

Fresh fruit in season   50p

# Table d'hôte

A table d'hôte menu, be it breakfast, lunch or dinner, usually offers a three or four course meal at a set price. Dishes from the recipe manual are used to compile the menu, and by utilising the appropriate dish costing card, and preparing a multiple cost sheet, an accurate food cost for the menu is quickly ascertained. If no choice is offered, the total cost of one portion of each course is used as the basis for calculating the menu price:

*Example 9:*

### TABLE D'HÔTE LUNCHEON
(3 course)

Cream of green pea soup
Chicken casserole
Boiled potatoes
Carrots Vichy
Fruit salad
Coffee extra 20p

*Multiple cost sheet*

Date: . . . . . . . . . . .

Menu: Cream of green pea soup
       Chicken casserole
       Boiled potatoes
       Carrots Vichy
       Fruit salad

| Portion | Dish | Cost of one portion | Revised costing | Revised costing | Revised costing |
|---|---|---|---|---|---|
| | | £ | | | |
| 1 | Cream of green pea soup | 0·08 | | | |
| 1 | Chicken casserole | 0·33 | | | |
| 1 | Boiled potatoes | 0·04 | | | |
| 1 | Carrots Vichy | 0·03 | | | |
| 1 | Fruit salad | 0·12 | | | |
| | | 0·60 | | | |

| | | | | | |
|---|---|---|---|---|---|
| Date | Menu minimum price @ 55% | 1·34 | | | |
| 1.4.19 .. | @ 60% | 1·50 | | | |
| | @ 65% | 1·72 | | | |

(Gross profit to nearest penny)

If there is a choice offered on a table d'hôte menu, the selection of dishes included in each course should have the same average basic food cost within a marginal percentage, to ensure the required gross profit margin is achieved:

*Example 10:*

### TABLE D'HÔTE DINNER MENU

£2·50

Consommé Mercedes
or
Crème St. Germain

Deep fried fillets of plaice, Sauce Tartare
or
Roast Duckling à l'orange
Croquettes, new, french fried potatoes
Fresh cauliflower au gratin
Fresh runner beans

Bread and butter pudding
or
Crème caramel

Coffee 20p

If 65% gross profit margin is expected from this menu, whatever selection of course is made, the food cost for one cover should not exceed:

$$\frac{35}{100} \times \frac{£2·50}{1} = \frac{£1·75}{2} = 87·5p$$

# Variety and appeal of menu

The compilation of the menu requires skill, judgement, experience and a thorough understanding of the basic principles of good menu planning and due consideration of the following factors:

1. The type of establishment
2. The type of people to be catered for
3. The type of menu to be offered, e.g. à la carte, table d'hôte, special functions
4. The seasonal availability of supplies
5. The overall balance of the menu with regard to ingredients, colour, food value

The caterer will aim to offer as wide as possible variety of menus in order to stimulate and keep the interest of his customers in the establishment. The recipes of certain expensive dishes, when costed and marked up to give the required profit margin, would result in the selling price exceeding the normal fixed menu price. In this instance the caterer has a choice of actions to take:

1. The recipe and/or the portion size of the dish can be reviewed to see if the basic food cost can be reduced without losing food and presentation value.
2. The cost per portion may remain unaltered but a lower gross profit margin is accepted on the dish.
3. The caterer can accept a lower profit margin on the expensive main-course dishes but, when planning the menu, this can be compensated by including the dish with starter, vegetable and sweet courses which can yield above-average or high profit margins. The net result will be the overall average percentage from the whole menu required by the caterer.

# Special functions

Banquets, wedding receptions, special parties, conferences and special functions are an additional source of income and can be very profitable business, but the caterer has to offer good food and service at a competitive price if he wishes to compete in this market.

## Calculation of charge per cover

1. Standard menus for every type of function and range of prices are costed on multiple cost sheets.
2. A selection of menus is offered to the client, or, if requested, a special menu can be constructed to the client's requirements, the cost of each dish being obtained from the unit cost card, and the total food cost of one cover calculated, and multiplied by the number of guests to be catered for.
3. Concentration of service over a short period of time to a large number of guests may require extra labour. The wages for any additional staff have to be calculated and included in the cost.
4. A percentage of the charge per cover has to be allowed to cover the cost of overheads.
5. The management decide what net profit percentage they aim to achieve from the function.

From this information it is possible to calculate what charge per cover will be made to enable the caterer to cover the food cost, additional labour, contribute to the overheads and make a reasonable percentage net profit.

*Example 11:*

The food cost for a special function for 100 covers is calculated from the menu selected to be £1·35 per cover. The additional labour cost will be £69. It is management policy that overheads should be provided for on the basis of 20% of sales, and a net profit of 12% should be achieved.

*Calculation of charge per cover—Special function—100 covers*

|  | £ | % of sales |
|---|---|---|
| Food cost—100 × £1·35 | 135·00 | |
| Additional labour | 69·00 | |
| Overheads | ? | 20% |
| Net profit | ? | 12% |
| Total charge | ? | 100% |

Total of food cost and additional labour:

   £135·00 + £69·00 = £204·00

Thus £204 represents 68% of sales (100%)
   £204·00 ÷ 68 = 1%, multiplied by 100
             = Total sales figure 100%

$$\frac{£204 \times 100}{68} = £300$$

*Charge per cover:*   £300 ÷ 100 = £3·00

*Overheads*   $\dfrac{20\%}{100} \times \dfrac{£300}{1} = £60$

*Net profit*   $\dfrac{12\%}{100} \times \dfrac{£300}{1} = £36$

*Food cost* as a percentage of sales:   $\dfrac{£135}{300} \times \dfrac{£100}{1} = 45\%$

*Additional labour* as a percentage of sales:   $\dfrac{£69}{300} \times \dfrac{100}{1} = 23\%$

|  | £ | % of sales |
|---|---|---|
| Food cost | 135·00 | 45% |
| Additional labour | 69·00 | 23% |
| Overheads | 60·00 | 20% |
| Net profit | 36·00 | 12% |
| Total charge | £300·00 | 100% |

*Charge per cover: £3·00*

If the establishment is asked to quote a charge per cover which will include additional items, such as floral decorations, hire of entertainers, band, toastmaster, and other miscellaneous items, the same principle is applied to calculate the charge per cover.

*Example 12:*

A dinner is to be arranged for 60 covers. A specially constructed menu has been costed and the total food cost is £138·00, additional labour £42, floral decorations £9, printing of special menus and place cards £10, toastmaster and orchestra £32. The management wishes to allocate $17\frac{1}{2}\%$ of sales for overheads, and achieve a net profit of $12\frac{1}{2}\%$.

*Dinner for 60 covers*

|  | £ | % of sales |
|---|---|---|
| Food cost | 138·00 | |
| Additional labour | 42·00 | |
| Floral decorations | 9·00 | 70 |
| Printing for special menu | 10·00 | |
| Toastmaster and orchestra | 32·00 | |
|  | 231·00 | |
| Overheads | ? | $17\frac{1}{2}$ |
| Net profit | ? | $12\frac{1}{2}$ |
| Total charge | ? | 100% |

The food cost, additional labour and extra items total £231, which represents 70% of the sales (100%):

$$\frac{£231}{70} = 1\% \quad \text{Multiply by } 100 = \text{total sales figure (100\%)}$$

Total sales: $\dfrac{£231}{70} \times \dfrac{100}{1} = \dfrac{£2,310}{7} = £330$

Charge per cover: $\dfrac{£330}{60} = £5·50$

£

Overheads: $\dfrac{17\frac{1}{2}\%}{100} \times \dfrac{£330}{1}$

|  |  |
|---|---|
| 10% | 33·00 |
| + 5% | 16·50 |
| + $2\frac{1}{2}\%$ | 8·25 |
| $17\frac{1}{2}\%$ | 57·75 |

Net profit: $\dfrac{12\frac{1}{2}\%}{100} \times \dfrac{£330}{1} = 8\overline{)330}$

£41·25

Food cost as a percentage of sales:

$$\frac{\overset{46}{£\cancel{138}}}{£\cancel{330}} \times 10\cancel{0} = 11\overline{)460}\ (41 \cdot 8\%$$

$$\begin{array}{r} 44 \\ \hline 20 \\ 11 \\ \hline 90 \\ 88 \\ \hline 2 \end{array}$$

Additional labour as a percentage of sales:

$$\frac{\overset{14}{£\cancel{44}}}{£\cancel{330}} \times 10\cancel{0} = 11\overline{)140}\ (12 \cdot 7\%$$

$$\begin{array}{r} 11 \\ \hline 30 \\ 22 \\ \hline 80 \\ 77 \\ \hline 3 \end{array}$$

| Floral decorations | £9·00 |
|---|---|
| Printing of special menus | £10·00 |
| Toastmaster and orchestra | £32·00 |
| | £51·00 |

as percentage of sales:

$$\frac{\overset{17}{£\cancel{51}}}{£\cancel{330}} \times 10\cancel{0} = 11\overline{)170}\ (15 \cdot 5\%\ \text{(to one decimal place)}$$

$$\begin{array}{r} 11 \\ \hline 60 \\ 55 \\ \hline 50 \end{array}$$

*Solution: Dinner for 60 covers*

| | £ | % of sales |
|---|---|---|
| Food cost | 138·00 | 41·8 |
| Additional labour | 42·00 | 12·7 |
| Floral decorations, printing of special menus, toastmaster and orchestra: | 51·00 | 15·5 |
| Overheads | 57·75 | 17·5 |
| Net profit | 41·25 | 12·5 |
| Total charge | £330·00 | 100·0% |

*Charge per cover: £5·50*

Unless the charge per cover specifically includes the provision of beverages, wines and spirits are costed and marked-up to be sold at the usual percentage gross profit margin (see Part 2, Chapter 9) as a separate charge.

# Progress test questions

1. Discuss the objects and advantages of the caterer compiling a recipe manual.

2. Using current price lists for unit value prices, prepare unit cost cards, showing the cost of one portion and selling price at 60% gross profit, from the following recipes:

(a)                      KIDNEY SOUP—10 portions
YIELD: 2 quarts $(2\frac{1}{4}$ litres$)$

| | | |
|---|---|---|
| 5 pints | Brown stock | 3 litres |
| 12 oz | Ox kidney | 340 grammes |
| 8 oz | Carrots | 225 grammes |
| 8 oz | Onions | 225 grammes |
| 3 oz | Flour | 85 grammes |
| 3 oz | Meat dripping | 85 grammes |
| 2 oz | Tomato purée | 60 grammes |
| $\frac{1}{2}$ oz | Salt | 15 grammes |
| | White pepper | 2 grammes |
| small | Bouquet garni | small |

(b)                        IRISH STEW
YIELD: 8 portions

| | | |
|---|---|---|
| $2\frac{1}{2}$ lb | Stewing lamb | 1·1 kg |
| 8 oz | White cabbage | 225 grammes |
| 8 oz | Leeks | 225 grammes |
| 6 oz | Celery | 170 grammes |
| 8 oz | Onions | 225 grammes |
| 8 oz | Button onions | 225 grammes |
| 2 lb | Potatoes | 0·9 kg |
| $\frac{1}{4}$ oz | Chopped parsley | 10 grammes |
| $\frac{1}{2}$ oz | Salt | 15 grammes |
| | Pepper | 2 grammes |
| 1 | Bouquet garni | 1 |
| 2 pints | Water | 1·1 litres |

3. From the sample à la carte menu on page 54 calculate the food cost of the following items if the restaurant is operating on a 65% gross profit margin:

    (a) Prawn cocktail
    (b) Spaghetti bolognaise
    (c) Scampi meunière
    (d) Lamb chop tyrolienne
    (e) Kidneys and bacon
    (f) Orange salad and kirsch

4. Prepare unit cost cards of the following dishes and from them compile a multiple cost sheet, for the table d'hôte 4-course menu. Calculate the food cost of one cover, and the menu price at (a) 55% gross profit margin; (b) 60% gross profit margin; (c) 65% gross profit margin:

    Consommé Julienne

    Scampi provençale

    Roast demi-poussin
    Bread sauce

    Garden peas
    Parisienne potatoes

    Raspberry Syllabub

5. Prepare unit cost cards of the following dishes and from them compile a multiple cost sheet for the table d'hôte 3-course menu. Calculate the food cost of one cover and the menu price at (a) 52% gross profit margin; (b) 63% gross profit margin; (c) 68% gross profit margin:

    Cream of tomato soup

    Entrecôte steak chasseur
    New potatoes
    Petit pois au beurre

    Sherry Trifle

6. Due to rising prices, a caterer finds that certain main course dishes when marked up to give the required gross profit percentage now exceed the normal fixed menu price. Suggest what courses of action should be considered by the caterer if he wishes to avoid increasing his menu prices.

7. A special function has been arranged for 100 covers. The food cost for the menu chosen will be £1·25 per head. Wages for extra staff will be £50. The management expect 20% of the sales to cover overheads, and require a net profit of 10%. Prepare a statement to show:

    (a) The charge per cover to the customer;

(b) The labour cost as a percentage of sales;
(c) The food cost as a percentage of sales;
(d) The amount of money is contributed to overheads;
(e) What amount of money the net profit percentage represents.

8. The total sales return from a special dinner for 130 covers amounts to £455.

(a) Calculate the charge per cover to the customer.
(b) The food cost amounts to £182·00. What percentage of the sales figure does this represent?
(c) The labour cost amounts to £113·75. What percentage of the sales figure does this represent?
(d) The management require 23% of the sales to cover the contribution to overheads. What amount of money does this represent?
(e) What net profit is achieved in monetary and percentage terms?

9. A special banquet has been arranged for 75 covers. The total food cost for the special menu is calculated as £151·87½; additional labour will cost £67·50; floral decorations, special menus, and sundry extras will cost £16·87½. The Management wish 17% of the sales to be allocated for overheads, and require to achieve a 13% net profit.

(a) Calculate the charge per cover to the customer.
(b) Prepare a statement to show:

(i) Food cost as a percentage of sales;
(ii) Labour cost as a percentage of sales;
(iii) Overheads allocation in monetary terms;
(iv) The net profit in monetary terms.

# CHAPTER 5

# Meat Costing

## Meat costing

By comparing costs the caterer will decide which is the most suitable and economical method of purchasing meat for his own particular establishment. If it is decided to purchase meat in a pre-portioned form, portion control and costing is relatively simple, but it must be remembered that the price of pre-portioned commodities will reflect the producer's cost of labour and packaging and could prove a more costly method of buying. In large-scale catering it could be more to the caterer's advantage to purchase meats in large joints or wholesale cuts which are butchered and portioned on the premises.

## *Portion control—meats*

Pre-portioned steaks, chops, steaklets and hamburgers are normally purchased at a higher price per kilogramme, which is a reflection of the labour involved in cutting and portioning the meat to size, but as the caterer may be able to save time and labour in the kitchen by using the pre-portioned meat, the increase in the food cost could be offset by a decrease in labour or overheads costs. However, if the food cost is increased the gross profit margin will be reduced if the selling price remains the same:

*Example 1:*
  *225 g fillet steak butchered and portioned in kitchen*

|  | £ | % of selling price |
|---|---|---|
| Cooked meat cost | 0·80 | 40 |
| Cost of labour for preparation | 0·60 | 30 |
| Cost of overheads | 0·40 | 20 |
| Net profit | 0·20 | 10 |
| Selling price | £2·00 | 100% |

Gross profit = Selling price − Food cost
£1·20 (60%) = £2·00 (100%) − £0·80 (40%)

*225 g fillet steak purchased pre-portioned*

|  | £ | % of selling price |
|---|---|---|
| Cooked meat cost | 1·00 | 50 |
| Cost of labour for preparation | 0·40 | 20 |
| Cost of overheads | 0·40 | 20 |
| Net profit | 0·20 | 10 |
| Selling price | £2·00 | 100% |

Gross profit = Selling price − Food cost
£1·00 (50%) = £2·00 (100%) − £1·00 (50%)

In this example, if pre-portioned meat is used, unless there is a 10% decrease between either labour or overhead costs, then the caterer will not achieve his 10% net profit if the selling price is to remain at £2·00. If the labour and overheads costs remain the same, to achieve 60% gross profit margin and a 10% net profit the pre-portion steak would have to be sold at:

$$\frac{\text{Food cost} \times 20}{8} = \frac{100 \times 20}{8} = £2·50$$

# Wholesale cuts

As the cost price of a portion of cooked meat is the basis for the calculation of the selling price, there are certain factors that have to be taken into consideration when the caterer purchases wholesale cuts.

1. As the wholesale cut is purchased at a set price per kg for the total weight, it is necessary to establish the price ratios between the different cuts of usable meat when the carcass is butchered; otherwise it would result in the selling price of all cuts being the same, for example entrecôte steak being sold at the same price as stewing meat.
2. The bone and cooking loss of the meat will have to be established in order to be able to calculate the cost price of the cooked meat.
3. Portion sizes of cooked meat to be served will have to be established in order to be able to calculate the selling price at a given gross profit percentage.

## Price ratios between different cuts

Butcher's meat is purchased in the following units:

| Beef | Joint, quarter or side |
|---|---|
| Lamb | Joint or carcass |
| Mutton | Joint or carcass |
| Pork | Joint, carcass or side |
| Veal | Joint, carcass or side |

When butchered the following joints are produced:

## Beef

*Hindquarter*—Average weight approximately 73 kg (160 lb)

JOINTS
Fillet
Rump
Shin
Silverside
Sirloin
Thin flank
Thick flank
Topside
Wing Rib

*Forequarter*—Average weight approximately 61 kg (135 lb)

JOINTS
Chuck ribs
Fore ribs
Middle ribs
Plate and brisket
Leg of mutton cut
Shank
Sticking piece

Fig. 5.1    Beef: side, forequarter and hindquarter

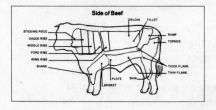

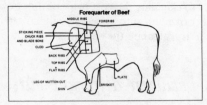

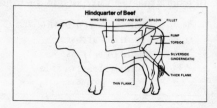

## Lamb

Average weight approximately 13–18 kg (30–40 lb)

## Mutton

Average weight approximately 18–23 kg (40–50 lb)

JOINTS

| | |
|---|---|
| Best end | Leg |
| Breast | Loin |
| Chop | Middle neck |
| Cutlet | Saddle |
| Fillet | Scrag end |

Fig. 5.2 Carcass of lamb

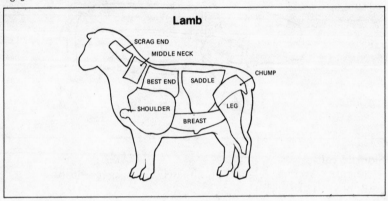

## Side of Pork

Average weight approximately 18–23 kg (40–50 lb)

JOINTS

| | |
|---|---|
| Belly | Shoulder |
| Leg | Spare rib |
| Loin | |

Fig. 5.3 Side of pork

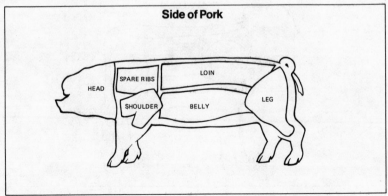

## Side of Bacon

Average weight approximately 25–30 kg (56–65 lb)

JOINTS

| | |
|---|---|
| Back | Hock |
| Collar | Streaky |
| Gammon | |

Fig. 5.4  Side of bacon

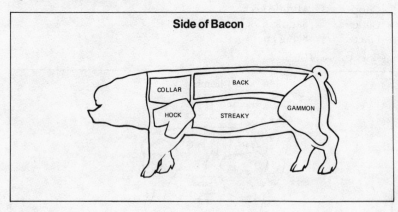

## Side of Veal

(English)  Average weight approximately 24–30 kg (53–66 lb)
(Bobby)  15 kg (33 lb)
(Dutch)  33–42 kg (73–93 lb)

JOINTS

| | |
|---|---|
| Best end | Loin |
| Breast | Neck end |
| Knuckle | Scrag |
| Leg | Shoulder |

Fig. 5.5  Side of veal

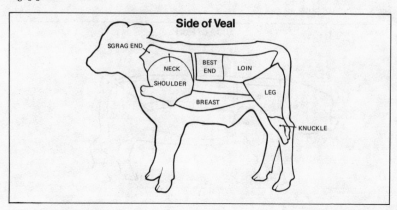

**Establishing price ratios between different cuts:**

*Example 2:*

A wholesale carcass of lamb weighing 15 kg (approx. 32 lb) is purchased at 85p per kg.

Total wholesale cost for 15 kg @ 85p per kg = £12·75.

When it is butchered it produces the following cuts:

|  | *Approx. weight* kg | *Approx. weight* lb |
|---|---|---|
| Best end | 2·0 | (4) |
| Breast | 1·5 | (3) |
| Leg | 3·25 | (7) |
| Middle neck | 2·0 | (4) |
| Scrag | 0·5 | (1) |
| Shoulders | 2·5 | (6) |
| Saddle | 3·25 | (7) |
|  | 15·0 kg | (32 lb) |

As the retail price for the following cuts would normally be less than the overall wholesale price per kg, they are deducted from the total weight and cost:

|  | kg | £ |
|---|---|---|
| Breast | 1·5 @ 50p per kg | 0·75 |
| Middle neck | 2·0 @ 60p per kg | 1·20 |
| Scrag end | 0·5 @ 60p per kg | 0·30 |
|  | 4·0 | 2·25 |

| | |
|---|---|
| Total wholesale cost | 12·75 |
| *Less* Cost of breasts, middle neck and scrag end | 2·25 |
| Total cost of remaining joints | £10·50 |

If the remaining cuts were purchased at the normal retail price per kg, the total retail cost would be as follows:

|  |  |  | £ |
|---|---|---|---|
| 2 kg | Best end | @ 133p per kilo | 2·66 |
| 3·25 kg | Leg | @ 144p per kilo | 4·68 |
| 2·5 kg | Shoulder | @ 90p per kilo | 2·25 |
| 3·25 kg | Saddle | @ 128p per kilo | 4·16 |
| 11·0 kg | | | 13·75 |

To calculate the price ratios between the different cuts the following formula should be used:

$$\frac{\text{Total wholesale cost} \times \text{Retail price per kg}}{\text{Total retail cost}}$$

$$\text{Best end} \qquad \frac{£10 \cdot 50}{£13 \cdot 75} \times \frac{133}{1} = 101 \cdot 6\text{p} \ (£1 \cdot 02 \text{ per kilo})$$

$$\text{Leg} \qquad \frac{£10 \cdot 50}{£13 \cdot 75} \times \frac{144}{1} = 110 \cdot 0\text{p} \ (£1 \cdot 10 \text{ per kilo})$$

$$\text{Shoulder} \qquad \frac{£10 \cdot 50}{£13 \cdot 75} \times \frac{90}{1} = 68 \cdot 7\text{p} \ (69\text{p per kilo})$$

$$\text{Saddle} \qquad \frac{£10 \cdot 50}{£13 \cdot 75} \times \frac{128}{1} = 97 \cdot 8\text{p} \ (98\text{p per kilo})$$

Having calculated the raw meat price ratio between the different cuts of meat, the next consideration is the calculation of the cooked meat price per kg, and the cooked meat price per portion. The amount of loss due to boning, trimming and cooking has to be calculated, for the total weight served is not the same as the total weight purchased, and the loss in weight has been paid for.

# Bone and cooking loss

The trimming, boning and cooking loss of meat is usually calculated as a percentage of the weight of the raw meat purchased. Regular checking will standardise the average percentages of loss, and kitchen procedures should be laid down and adhered to by the staff on the treatment of meat so that any unusual variances in the percentages will be noted.

## Treatment of meat

1. The joint of meat is weighed before cooking.
2. The joint of meat is weighed after cooking.
3. The cooking loss as a percentage is calculated.

*Example 3:*

| | |
|---|---|
| Joint before cooking | 8·0 kg |
| Joint after cooking | 6·5 kg |
| Cooking loss | 1·5 kg |

Cooking loss as a percentage of raw meat:

$$\frac{1 \cdot 5}{8} \times \frac{100}{1} = 18 \cdot 75\%$$

4. After carving the bones and scraps are weighed to establish trimming and bone loss.

*Example 4:*

| Raw meat weight | 8·0 kg |
| Weight of bones and scraps | 2·0 kg |

Weight of bone and scrap loss as a percentage of raw meat:

$$\frac{2}{8} \times \frac{100}{1} = 25\%$$

| Cooking loss | 1·5 kg | (18·75%) |
| Bone and scrap loss | 2·0 kg | (25·00%) |
| Bone and cooking loss | 3·5 kg | (43·75%) |

| Weight of usable cooked meat: | 8·0 kg | (100·00%) |
| *less* | 3·5 kg | ( 43·75%) |
| | 4·5 kg | ( 56·25%) |

5. If the standard portion of cooked meat to be served is 150 grammes, the carver has the responsibility of producing 4·5 kg ÷ 150 grammes = 450 ÷ 15 = 30 portions.

# Cooked meat price

*To calculate the price per kg and price per portion of the served meat the following formulas can be used:*

1. Served meat price per kg

$$= \frac{\text{Weight of raw meat} \times \text{raw meat price per kilogramme}}{\text{Weight of usable cooked meat}}$$

2. Served meat price per kg

$$= \frac{\text{Raw meat price per kilogramme} \times 100}{\text{Usable cooked meat percentage of raw meat}}$$

e.g. If 45% of the raw meat is lost by bone and cooking loss, the usable cooked meat percentage of raw meat left is 55%.

3. Served meat price per portion

$$= \frac{\text{Weight of raw meat} \times \text{raw meat price per kg}}{\text{Number of portions of cooked meat served}}$$

*Example 5:*

A joint weighing 10 kg is purchased at 120p per kg. The bone and cooking loss is 40%. Calculate:

(a) The price per kg of served meat;
(b) The number of 150 g portions obtainable from the carved meat;
(c) The cost per portion of cooked meat;
(d) The selling price of one 150 g portion of cooked meat at a 65% gross profit margin.

*Solution*

(a) *Using Formula 2*—Served meat price per kg

$$= \frac{120p \times 100}{60\%} = 200p \text{ per kg}$$

*Using Formula 1*—Served meat price per kg

$$= \frac{10 \text{ kg} \times 120p}{6 \text{ kg}} = 200p \text{ per kg}$$

(b) If the bone and cooking loss is 40%, the remaining weight of cooked meat = 60% of 10 kg

$$= \frac{60}{100} \times \frac{10}{1} = 6 \text{ kg}$$

(c) Number of 150 g portions of served meat obtainable from 6 kg

$$= \frac{6,000}{150} = 40 \times 150 \text{ g portions}$$

*Using Formula 3*—Served meat price per portion

$$= \frac{10 \text{ kg} \times 120p}{40} = 30p \text{ per portion}$$

(d) To calculate the selling price of one 150 g portion of served meat at 65% gross profit margin: $\dfrac{\text{Cost price} \times 20}{7}$

$$= \frac{30p \times 20}{7} = \frac{600}{7} = 85 \cdot 7p \text{ per portion (86p to nearest}$$
whole penny)

*Example 6:*

A wholesale cut weighing 23 kg (rump and loin without flank, kidney and suet) is purchased at 120p per kg. The chef has boned and trimmed and the following cuts have been produced:

|  | kg |
|---|---|
| Fillet | 1·5 |
| Rump | 4·0 |
| Sirloin | 7·5 |
| Stewing meat | 5·0 |
| Bones | 4·5 |
| Waste | 0·5 |

The bones are priced at 20p per kg, and the stewing meat at 85p per kg. Find the cost of a served portion of:
(a) Fillet steak (250 g)
(b) Rump (125 g)
(c) Sirloin (125 g)

*Solution*
To find the price ratio of different cuts:

1. Total wholesale cost:
   23 kg × 120p per kg = £27·60
   Total wholesale weight, less

|                                        | £      |
|----------------------------------------|--------|
| Stewing meat, 5 kg @ 85p per kg        | 4·25   |
| Bones 4·5 kg @ 20p per kg              | 0·90   |
| Waste 0·5 kg                           | —      |
|                                        | £5·15  |

Total wholesale cost, less stewing meat, bones and wastage

$$= £27·60$$
$$\text{less} \quad 5·15$$
$$£22·45$$

Total retail cost of remaining joints:

|                                  |        |
|----------------------------------|--------|
| 1·5 kg Fillets @ 340p per kg     | 5·10   |
| 4·0 kg Rump @ 210p per kg        | 8·40   |
| 7·5 kg Sirloin @ 180p per kg     | 13·50  |
|                                  | £27·00 |

*Formula:* $\dfrac{\text{Total wholesale cost} \times \text{Retail price per kilo}}{\text{Total retail cost}}$

Fillet $= \dfrac{£22·45 \times £3·40}{£27·00} = 282·6\text{p per kg}$ (283p per kg to nearest penny)

Rump $= \dfrac{£22·45 \times £2·10}{£27·00} = 174·6\text{p per kg}$ (175p per kg)

Sirloin $= \dfrac{£22·45 \times £1·80}{£27·00} = 149·7\text{p per kg}$ (150p per kg)

Assuming a 35% average cooking loss, the weight of the remaining cooked meat equals 65% of the raw weight.

*Using Formula 2*

1. Fillet steak: $\dfrac{283\text{p per kg} \times 100}{65\%} = 435·4\text{p per kg}$

   ∴ A 250 g fillet steak would cost $\dfrac{435·4}{4} = 108·85\text{p per portion}$ (109p per portion to nearest penny)

2. One 125 g (1/8 kg) portion of rump steak

   $= \dfrac{175\text{p} \times 100}{8 \times 65} = \dfrac{269·2\text{p per kg}}{8} = 33·65 \text{ per portion}$ (34p to nearest penny)

3. One 125 g (1/8 kg) portion of sirloin

   $= \dfrac{150\text{p} \times 100}{8 \times 65} = \dfrac{230·7\text{p per kg}}{8} = 28·83 \text{ per portion}$ (29p to nearest penny)

If the management policy is to sell at a 60% gross profit margin, the following would be put on the menu at a minimum price of:

1. 250 g Fillet steak: Cost per portion $= \dfrac{\text{C.P.} \times 20}{8}$

$$= \dfrac{109 \times 20}{8} = 272 \cdot 5\text{p per portion} (£2 \cdot 73)$$

2. 125 g Rump steak: Cost per portion $= \dfrac{34 \times 20}{8} = 85\text{p per portion}$

3. 125 g Sirloin steak: Cost per portion $= \dfrac{29 \times 20}{8} = 72 \cdot 5\text{p per portion}$
(73p)

# Progress test questions

1. Explain the advantages and disadvantages of purchasing pre-portioned meat packs.

2. Why is it necessary to establish the price ratios between different cuts when purchasing wholesale cuts of meat?

3. What is meant by bone and cooking loss?

4. Explain why it is necessary to specify portion sizes of meat to be served and why portion control is essential.

5. A joint weighing 12 kg is purchased at 110p per kilogramme. After cooking and carving it produces 56 × 140 g portions. Calculate:

    (a) the cooking loss percentage; and
    (b) the cost of a portion of served meat.

6. A wholesale cut of fore-rib of beef weighs 10 kg and costs 95p per kilogramme. The trimmings and wastage when cut amount to 1 kg. The weight after cooking is 6 kg. After carving 53 × 100 g portions are served. Calculate:

    (a) the total wholesale cost of the joint;
    (b) the cooking loss in weight;
    (c) the cooking loss as a percentage of trimmed weight;
    (d) the total weight of served meat;
    (e) the total bone, cooking and trimming loss in weight and as a percentage of the gross wholesale cut;
    (f) the cost price per portion of served meat;
    (g) the selling price of a portion of served meat at a 60% gross profit margin;
    (h) the total selling price of 53 × 100 g portions;
    (i) the gross profit made in monetary terms.

# Part Two

# Areas of Control

# CHAPTER 6

# Cost Control

## The objects & advantages of cost control

In order to be effective, control work should always be up to the minute, as results more than a few hours old become ineffectual in their impact. Control work should enhance the efficiency of management and, if necessary, should result in action being taken to prevent fraud and inefficiency.

## *Advantages*

1. A simple cost control system will disclose the profitability of each revenue producing department.
2. Cost control can be exercised over all operations from the purchase of goods to accounting for sales.
3. An efficient system of cost control will reveal possible sources of economy and result in a rational utilisation of materials and labour.
4. Cost control provides the information necessary for the adoption of a sound pricing policy.
5. Cost control will facilitate speedy quotation for special functions such as banquets and wedding receptions.
6. Comparative results are easy with a cost control system, and comparisons with the industry as a whole can be facilitated.
7. Cost control data are an important instrument in the hands of management for making policy decisions.

## *Function of the cost controller*

It is the function of cost controllers:

1. To ensure that any cost control system is simple and adapted to the general pattern of the organisation;
2. To ensure the co-operation of all departments, so that the system will function correctly;
3. To ensure that all forms and procedures necessary for effective control are properly used and maintained;
4. To ensure that staff are instructed and assisted in the completion of control documents, bearing in mind that the majority of personnel may well be unfamiliar with them and not understand their purpose.

# The implementation of control

All members of staff should be cost and control-conscious, but some members of staff have the further responsibility of ensuring that cost control systems are implemented.

## 1. Managers/Assistant managers

Managers and their assistants have responsibility for the actions of the employees under them and are also expected to account for the profitability and effectiveness of the areas under their control.

## 2. Heads of departments

Heads of Departments are also responsible for the staff and for the efficiency and profitability of their Departments.

## 3. Control clerks

A knowledge of book-keeping procedures is an essential for control clerks, as the compilation of cost control data involves the completion of accountancy forms and documents used for the presentation of statistical material.

## 4. Storekeepers and stock controllers

Storekeepers and personnel handling stock must be responsible for all goods received in and out of stores, and for the records that have to be maintained for stock control purposes.

## 5. Accounts personnel and cash handlers

Personnel handling cash must account fully for all moneys involved in the course of transactions. Accounts personnel and clerks are expected to ensure that all transactions are properly recorded in the appropriate accounts and financial control documents.

# Areas of control

## 1. *Assets*

Staff must be aware that capital is invested in the assets of the business such as fixtures and fittings, china, plate, glassware, linen, stock of any description and cash in the hands of cashiers or other employees, and strict control over all assets must be maintained to ensure that they are not mishandled or misappropriated.

## 2. *Revenue*

Revenue control means that every time food, beverage, accommodation or any form of service is given, it will result in the sale being recorded either as cash in the till or as a charge on a customer's account.

## 3. *Food and beverage consumption*

Consumption control means that whenever food or beverage leaves the stores, it should result in a sale of the unit at a given percentage Gross Profit. Control commences with the purchase of supplies, their delivery to the correct department and consequential sale.

# The control pattern

Control work falls into three planes of activity.

## 1. *The primary plane*

**Food and beverages**

When a guest orders a meal at a hotel or restaurant the waiter or waitress records the food item on the waiter's check pad, and transmits the order to the kitchen. When drinks or beverage are ordered the waiter or wine waiter will take the order and record the item on his check pad, and then passes the order to the dispense bar or stillroom. It is essential that the items on these checks should result in a cash-paid bill or a charge on a customer's account.

On a routine daily basis, waiters' checks from the kitchen, stillroom, pastry larder, dispense bar and any other issuing points should be collected and sent to the food and beverage control office, where they will be matched with the duplicate copies of cash bills or charge bills received from the billing office.

The details of the day's business are entered on various summary and analysis sheets (these will be discussed in detail in later chapters) which are also forwarded to the food and beverage control office and are cross-checked against waiters' checks and bills from the billing office.

## Till readings

Food and beverage controllers must read every till between the end of the evening shift and the commencement of the next day's business. The till readings must be entered on the daily cash sheet and be agreed with the day's business analysis. When the till is read and cleared the machine should then be reset to zero by the controller.

Food and beverage control and till reading are primary-plane control routines and if a controller discovers any discrepancies, they must immediately report the matter to senior controllers, so that action can be taken and the matter investigated.

# 2. The secondary plane

The secondary plane of control concerns the continual audit and operation of cash, stock, overheads and labour control systems. Information and data from the summary and analysis sheets produced by the control systems are forwarded to senior controllers for use in the preparation of managerial reports, forecasts and budgets.

## Assets stock control

A complete inventory of all assets such as kitchen equipment and fixtures and fittings should be maintained and kept up to date. Stock record cards should be kept of all working assets, such as linen, china, plate and glassware. The stock record cards should show the standard amount of stock in use, and all breakages, replacements and renewals should be noted. Regular checks should be made on all stock and staff motivated to care for the valuable assets under their control.

## Labour control

Daily returns in respect of hours worked, including overtime by hourly paid staff, should be completed and signed by heads of sections, which should be vetted and countersigned by the controllers. From these returns weekly labour cost statements can be prepared. The information and data from these returns will establish whether the labour costs for each department are reasonable, and comparisons can be made with the estimated labour cost and original forecast.

## Overheads control

Operating expenses such as light, heat, fuel and power come under the heading of overhead costs and the control of such expenditure is the direct responsibility of the heads of departments. Regular checks on gas and electricity meters should be made and the units used noted; records of fuel and power consumption should be made and any deviation from the normal should be reported immediately, and an investigation made. Other overhead expenses such as printing and stationery, postage and telephone, cleaning materials and other sundry expenses, should also be under strict control. Stock record cards should be kept for all printing, stationery, advertising materials, and cleaning materials. Records should be kept of all postage and telephone expenses and any deviations from the normal expenditure on any of these items should be noted and checked.

## Revenue control

Revenue control means the accounting of issues of all food and drink supplied by the restaurants or bars resulting in cash in the till or as a credit charge on a customer's account. At the end of business, daily cash analysis and summary sheets should be prepared by cashiers and handed in with the cash to be doubled-checked by the controllers. Spot checks should be made regularly on tills and cash floats, and any discrepancies should be noted and dealt with immediately.

## Food and beverage control

All foodstuffs received, either directly into the kitchen, or by daily issues from the stores or cellars to the kitchen, should be recorded in an analysed kitchen day book. This analysis will provide up-to-the-minute figures for the calculation of the food cost percentages and also provide figures on the percentages spent on each type of commodity; thus control can be exercised over the food cost percentage and any deviations can be corrected quickly. A check analysis compiled from the checks handed in by the waiter will provide a breakdown of issues of food from the hotplate. The total of portions sold plus any portions left unsold should equal the anticipated yield from the quantities of materials going into the kitchen. Any discrepancies will call for immediate investigation. Similarly a beverage purchase breakdown book should be maintained by the cellar to provide overall control of all receipts and issues. Stock record cards should also be maintained in the cellar, and in addition a daily issues analysis showing the issues to each individual outlet, which, when totalled, can be transferred on to individual bar consumption summaries; thus control can be exercised throughout, and any discrepancies investigated.

## Stock control

Controllers should make regular spot checks on stores, cellar, and bars, physically counting residual stocks. Use should be made of the stock record card system by selecting a few random cards and proving the balance of the stock as shown by the card, against the physical count made by the controller. Any discrepancies noted require immediate action to be taken to find the cause.

# 3. *The tertiary plane*

It is the responsibility of the senior controllers to collate all the information and data compiled from primary and secondary control and prepare statistical reports in a form suitable for presentation to the management. If results differ from targets set, or if there are any particular problem areas, the senior controller should be able to interpret the situation and advise the management as to the cause and possibly the solution in that particular area of control. The following are some of the reports that have to be prepared.

### 1. Cost and sales report

This report is one of the most important documents prepared by the senior controllers. It informs management of the trading results of each outlet, e.g. bars and restaurants and room sales.

### 2. Stock turnover reports

This report is prepared to inform the management of the total value and rate of turnover of stock in stores and cellar.

### 3. Labour cost reports

This report details the labour cost requirements for each department.

### 4. Reconciliation of costs and sales

The object of this report is to ensure that the figures reported to the management are consistent with those recorded in the financial accounts.

### 5. Forecast reports

It is the responsibility of senior food and beverage controllers to prepare from the information and data supplied to them forecasts of revenue and labour for the various revenue-producing departments.

### 6. Food and beverage controllers' reports

It is the responsibility of senior controllers to ensure that procedures laid down by the management are adhered to, and that various reports, summaries, analysis sheets and other documentation is received by them on the appointed day and time. A food and beverage controller's report is prepared to highlight the results of their endeavours and general efficiency of all departments within their control area, and this report is usually circulated to the following:

Hotel General Manager
Restaurant Manager
Bars Manager
Banqueting Manager
Chief Accountant
and any other head of department directly concerned.

## PRIMARY PLANE CONTROL AREA

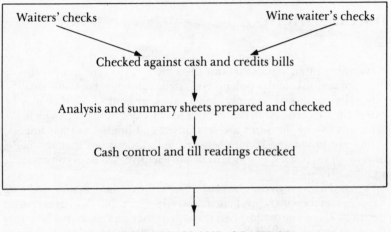

Waiters' checks      Wine waiter's checks

Checked against cash and credits bills

Analysis and summary sheets prepared and checked

Cash control and till readings checked

## SECONDARY PLANE CONTROL

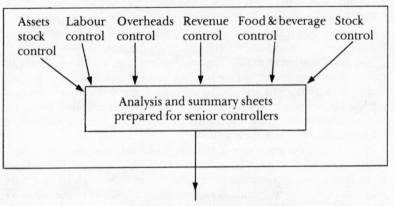

Assets stock control Labour control Overheads control Revenue control Food & beverage control Stock control

Analysis and summary sheets prepared for senior controllers

## TERTIARY PLANE CONTROL

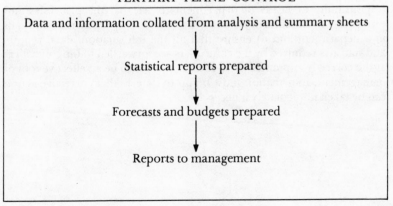

Data and information collated from analysis and summary sheets

Statistical reports prepared

Forecasts and budgets prepared

Reports to management

# Control as an effective aid to management

The caterer, to be successful, must stay alert to all the complex and constantly shifting trends that can affect his business. The trends must be analysed and risks and problems evaluated. Subsequent decisions may be internally concerned with personnel, costs, or control, or they may be externally concerned with competitive prices, expansion or changes in the sales mix. Some decisions are specialised and limited in their impact; others are broad and comprehensive; but all decisions that are made, internal or external, specialised or comprehensive, will be of considerable significance.

A wise decision can only be made after sufficient information and data have been gathered and evaluated; and effective, profitable management decisions cannot be made unless they are based on a system that furnishes the management with all the operating facts relating to their restaurant or hotel.

Cost control is interrelated to the accountancy cycle and a prerequisite for any cost controller is a sound basic knowledge of the double-entry book-keeping system and of accountancy procedures.

The first function of the accountancy system is to record accurately all the transactions of the business. This recorded information is then classified, summarised and evaluated, and from this summarised and analysed information the management will be able to measure the success of their operations, attack fraud and inefficiency and forecast and budget for future operations and expansions.

As an establishment grows in size the problems grow proportionately larger and more complex. In order that it can be effectively directed and controlled as a unit, the management sub-divides the establishment into major and minor departments and imposes a control system network designed to organise and control the activity of each department. It is the responsibility of heads of department to see that the principles and procedures of the control systems are adhered to by the members of staff in a department and to ensure that all the information, data, reports and statistics required by the controllers are forwarded to the controllers at the correctly appointed time, for if control is to be an effective tool of management, information must be up to date so that corrective action can be taken immediately if necessary.

# Progress test questions

1. What are the objects and advantages of cost control systems?

2. What is the function of the cost controller?

3. Which personnel have special responsibilities for the implementation of control procedures?

4. Define the areas of control.

5. Define the three planes of activity in the control pattern.

6. Discuss the statement 'Control must be used as an effective tool of management'.

# CHAPTER 7

# Food Control

## The stock control system

Most establishments provide good security for their cash but fail to realise that a great deal more money can be tied up in stock; therefore the security of stock is the essence of good control. The best system of stock control is the most simple one, easily understood by the staff operating it, and easy to implement. It must be made to suit the nature and the size of the business, and the possibilities of error must be reduced to a minimum.

Stock should be kept at its lowest workable level, as overstocking can result in loss in value through spoilage; also excessive stock immobilises large amounts of capital, making it impossible to maintain a profitable rate of return on that capital.

A good stock control system will provide:

1. The control over the movement of stock in and out of stores.
2. Control over the level of stocks.
3. Stock records from which information can be easily extracted, regarding orders placed, materials received and issues made from the stores.

## The duties and responsibilities of the storekeeper

The storekeeper holds a very responsible position in any establishment. The extent of his responsibility will depend on the size and nature of the business. In smaller establishments the storekeeper may be responsible for ordering, receiving, issuing and keeping all stock records. In large establishments a buyer would place all orders, a receiving clerk would check and receive goods into stores, stock clerks would issue goods and keep the records, and the head storekeeper would have overall responsibility and be expected to produce reports and statistics for the food and beverage controllers. Irrespective of whether there is one storekeeper performing all duties, or several members of a storekeeping staff, the following tasks will have to be dealt with in the control network:

1. Supplies have to be ordered.
2. When the goods are received, they must be checked against the copy order (Fig. 7.2) and delivery notes (Fig. 7.3).
3. The goods must be binned and entered on the 'bin cards' (Fig. 7.8).
4. The delivery notes and copy orders are 'married together' and the goods received book (Fig. 7.7) is written up from the delivery note.
5. When the invoice (Fig. 7.4) arrives, it is checked against the delivery note and order copy. Prices and calculations are checked and the goods entered on the stock record cards (Fig. 7.9).
6. If all is correct the invoice is passed for payment to the accounts department, where it is used to write up a purchases day book.
7. When goods are required by any of the other departments, a departmental requisition (Fig. 7.10) has to be completed, signed by an authorised person and passed to the stores, where the storekeeper will supply the goods according to the requisition.
8. The requisition is used to book the goods 'out' on the bin card and stock record cards.
9. An issues analysis (Fig. 7.11) is prepared from the requisitions, which is then forwarded to the food and beverage controller for statistical reports and analysis.

# Documents used in control of ordering

Orders for perishable goods are usually made on a daily basis by telephone to enable the wholesaler to 'shop' for fresh foods for delivery the following day.

Orders for dry goods are usually made on a re-order basis, which means that when the stock reaches the re-order point as stated on the stock record card or bin card, an order is placed. The other method of ordering is for the stock usage of the commodity to be calculated, and automatic periodical orders placed.

## Suppliers

A card index should be maintained showing details of all suppliers, the name, address, telephone numbers, terms given such as trade and cash discounts, delivery dates and any other relevant information that is necessary. Whilst it is normal to have one or two suppliers, it is important for the buyer to check alternative sources of supply regularly for competitive prices and new products. It is essential that good communication with suppliers is maintained so that any price changes are noted immediately.

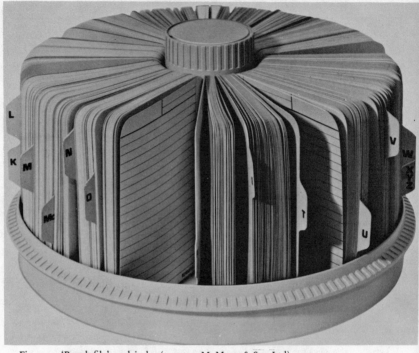

Fig. 7.1 'Rondofile' card-index (courtesy M. Myers & Son Ltd)

## Catalogues and price lists

Suppliers' catalogues and price lists should be filed in chronological order, the most recent on the top. Stock controllers should ensure that any price changes are notified to all revenue-producing departments, and that all stock records are amended.

## Order forms (Fig. 7.2)

These forms are official documents which are usually printed with the name of the establishment and numbered consecutively. If for any reason an order form is spoilt, it should not be destroyed but the word 'cancelled' should be written across the face and it should be filed in its numerical order.

Order forms for goods for stock are usually in sets, the top copy being white and any other copies which the management require for distribution are coloured for easy identification, e.g.:

| | | |
|---|---|---|
| *Copy* 1 | WHITE | Supplier |
| *Copy* 2 | PINK | Accounts |

| Copy 3 | BLUE | Food and beverage controller |
| Copy 4 | YELLOW | Stores |
| Copy 5 | GREEN | Departmental buyer |
| Copy 6 | WHITE | Head Office |

As orders for perishable goods are telephoned, a copy of the order is written on an official order set and distributed to:

| Copy 1 | WHITE | Receiving department |
| Copy 2 | BLUE | Food and beverage controller |
| Copy 3 | GREEN | Buyer |
| Copy 4 | PINK | Accounts |

The number of copies and colours are decided by the management to meet their own particular requirements.

## Essential details of a purchase order

1. Order Number
2. Date
3. Supplier's name and address
4. Quantity
5. Description of goods ordered
6. Unit
7. Quantity received
8. Unit price
9. Value
10. Signature of authorised person
11. Distribution

Fig. 7.2   Purchase order

**Purchase Order**

JAMESVILLE HOTELS LIMITED
EASTGATE
TELEPHONE EASTGATE 569

TO   A. Supplier Limited
West Lane
London EC2

③

① NUMBER   62

② DATE   2.1.1977

| ④ QUANTITY | ⑥ UNIT | ⑤ DESCRIPTION | ⑧ UNIT VALUE | ⑨ VALUE | ⑦ QUANTITY RECEIVED |
|---|---|---|---|---|---|
| 2 | 12x3½oz(99g) | Mustard | 1.64 | 3.28 | |
| 3 | 24 x large | Evaporated Milk | 2.97 | 8.91 | |

DISTRIBUTION ⑪
PINK          GREEN
BLUE          YELLOW
              WHITE

⑩ SIGNATURE OF AUTHORISED PERSON

91

# Delivery notes (Fig. 7.3)

When goods arrive they are usually accompanied by a delivery note, which is the supplier's covering note of goods supplied. The receiving clerk should check the goods against the details on the delivery note and the copy order. If the goods delivered agree with these two documents, the clerk will sign for what he has received. If the goods are not as ordered they should be rejected. If it is only the quantity that is short the copy order should be amended to the quantity received, and the delivery note should be only signed for this quantity. Further part-orders received are marked off the same copy order.

Fig. 7.3   Delivery note

| CUSTOMERS COPY | | **Delivery Note** | | | |
|---|---|---|---|---|---|
| TO Jamesville Hotel Ltd<br>Eastgate<br>London W2 | | A. SUPPLIER LIMITED<br>WEST LANE<br>LONDON EC2<br>TELEPHONE 01-224 7624 | | NUMBER 54340<br><br>DATE  12. 1. 19 | |
| PLEASE RECEIVE IN GOOD CONDITION: | | | | | |
| ORDER<br>NUMBER | QUANTITY | DESCRIPTION | UNIT<br>VALUE | REMARKS | |
| 62 | 2x12x99g<br>3x24x1large | Mustard<br>Evaporated Milk | | | |
| DELIVERED BY | | | RECEIVED BY | | |
| SIGNATURE | | | SIGNATURE | | |

# Invoices (Fig. 7.4)

An invoice is sent by the supplier to the customer and is a detailed account of goods sold. It is numbered and shows the quantity, quality, description, unit value and prices of the goods, including any charges for containers or delivery. The details on the invoice are checked against the delivery note and copy order. At the end of each week the invoice numbers are entered on a control list and sent with delivery notes and copy orders to the food and beverage controllers.

# *Statements* (Fig. 7.5)

A statement is a summarised account sent by the supplier to the customer, usually at the end of each month. It shows the purchases during that month plus any amounts owing at the beginning of the month, deducting any returns, discounts or payments made. It shows the balance due and is notification that payment is due. Invoices and credit notes received should be checked against the statement before it is passed for payment by the accounts department.

Fig. 7.5   Statement

**Statement**

TO: Jamesville Hotel
Eastgate
London W2

A. SUPPLIER LIMITED
WEST LANE
LONDON EC2
TELEPHONE 01-224 7624

ACCOUNT NUMBER 24

| DATE | REFERENCE | DEBIT | CREDIT | BALANCE |
|------|-----------|-------|--------|---------|
| 1977 | | | | |
| Jan 1 | Balance brought forward | | | 232.25 |
| 4 | Invoice 354 | 28.05 | | 260.30 |
| 6 | Invoice 490 | 14.95 | | 275.25 |
| 8 | Invoice 510 | 18.08 | | 293.33 |
| 9 | Cheque | | 90.73 | |
| | Discount | | 4.77 | 197.83 |
| 10 | Invoice 520 | 10.17 | | 208.00 |
| 11 | Credit Note 17 | | 5.20 | 202.80 |
| 12 | Invoice 523 | 6.24 | | 209.04 |

Fig. 7.4   Invoice

**Invoice**

NO. 5231
TAX POINT DATE 12.7.19..

TO Jamesville Hotel Ltd
Eastgate
London W2

A. SUPPLIER LIMITED
WEST LANE
LONDON EC2
TELEPHONE 01-224 7624

YOUR ORDER NUMBER 32    CARRIAGE   Van    TERMS   Trade Discount-20%

| CATALOGUE NUMBER | QUANTITY | DESCRIPTION | PRICE PER UNIT | £ | p | VAT RATE | VAT AMOUNT £ | p |
|------------------|----------|-------------|----------------|---|---|----------|--------------|---|
| | 2x1000 | Tea bags | 2.80 | 5. | 60 | 0 | — | — |
| | 2x2kilo | Pork Luncheon Meat | 1.10 | 2. | 20 | 0 | — | — |
| | | | | 7. | 80 | | — | — |
| | | Less: 20% trade discount | | 1. | 56 | | — | — |
| | | TOTAL | | 6. | 24 | | — | — |

TOTAL DUE  £6.24

93

# Credit notes (Fig. 7.6)

A credit note is a form, usually printed in red, sent by the supplier to the customer when goods have been returned. It shows that the customer's account has been credited with the amount involved. The credit note should be entered in the purchases returns book.

Fig. 7.6   Credit note—this is usually printed or typed in red

| | | | **Credit Note** | | NO.  37846 | | | |
|---|---|---|---|---|---|---|---|---|
| | | | | | TAX POINT DATE 24.7.19.. | | | |
| TO  Jamesville Hotel Ltd Eastgate London W2 | | | | | A.  SUPPLIER LIMITED WEST LANE LONDON EC2 TELEPHONE 01-224 7624 | | | |
| YOUR ORDER NUMBER   32 | | | INVOICE NUMBER   5231 | | TERMS Trade Dicount - 20% | | | |
| CATALOGUE NUMBER | QUANTITY | | DESCRIPTION | | PRICE PER UNIT | £        p | VAT RATE | VAT AMOUNT £      p |
| | 2x2kilo | | Pork Luncheon Meat | | 1.10 | 2.20 | 0 | –    – |
| | | | Less: 20% trade discount | | | 2.20 .44 | 0 | –    – |
| | | | | | TOTAL | 1.76 | | –    – |
| | | | | | | | TOTAL | £1.76 |

# Goods received book (Fig. 7.7)

A daily record of goods received into the stores is entered into a Goods Received Book from the delivery note. The date, supplier's name, copy order and delivery note, reference number and details of goods received are entered in the appropriate column, also any remarks regarding the order are made in the remarks column. On receipt of the invoice, unit value and prices can be entered.

Fig. 7.7   Goods received note

| | | | | **Goods Received Book** | | | |
|---|---|---|---|---|---|---|---|
| DATE | SUPPLIERS NAME | ORDER NUMBER | DELIVERY NOTE NUMBER | DETAILS | UNIT VALUE | VALUE | REMARKS |
| | | | | | | | |

# Stock control

## *Bin cards* (Fig. 7.8)

After goods have been checked against the delivery note and copy order, they are 'binned' by the storekeeper, which means that they are stored on the shelves or containers in the stock room particularly allocated to that commodity. A 'bin card' should be kept for every commodity. All receipts will be recorded direct from the suppliers' delivery notes on the day they are received into the stores, and all issues will be recorded daily from the requisitions from the various departments. The balance column on the bin card will increase when goods are received and decrease when goods are issued. The balance as shown on the bin card should be the same as the quantity on the shelves or in the bin. The maximum stock, minimum stock and re-order point will be decided by the food and beverage controller and will depend on the requirements of the establishment and availability.

Fig. 7.8   Bin card

### Bin Card

COMMODITY Evaporated milk   RE-ORDER POINT 3×24 (72 tins)   SUPPLIER
MAXIMUM STOCK 6×24 (144 tins)   BIN NUMBER 6
MINIMUM STOCK 2×24

| DATE | REFERENCE | RECEIVED | ISSUED | BALANCE |
|------|-----------|----------|--------|---------|
| 197.. | Balance brought forward | | | 28 |
| Jan 1 | Invoice No. 23 | 48 | | 76 |
| 1 | Requisition No. 22 | | 12 | 64 |
| 2 | Requisition No. 31 | | 24 | 40 |

## *Stock record cards* (Fig. 7.9)

The bin card records the quantities of goods received into and booked out of the stores. The stock record card also shows the monetary value of the goods booked into and out of the stores. The prices of the commodities are obtained from the invoices; the requisitions are costed and the value of goods going to the various departments are booked out. The value of the balance on the stock record card should be equal to the balance on the 'Bin Card'. Bin cards and stock record cards should be checked against each other for control purposes—the quantity recorded on the bin card should agree with that on the stock record card (small establishments combine the two).

**Stock Record Card**

BIN NUMBER  6

SUPPLIERS  1

COMMODITY  Evaporated milk

RE-ORDER QUANTITY  6 x 24

2

RE-ORDER LEVEL  3 x 24

| DATE 197— | REFERENCE | | UNIT COST | RECEIVED NO | RECEIVED £ | ISSUED NO | ISSUED £ | BALANCE NO | BALANCE £ |
|---|---|---|---|---|---|---|---|---|---|
| Jan 1 | | B/F | £0 12 | | | | | 28 | 3 36 |
| " 1 | Inv. no. 23 | | 0 12 | 48 | 5 76 | | | 76 | 9 12 |
| " 1 | Req'n no. 21 | | | | | 12 | 1 44 | 64 | 7 68 |
| " 2 | "  " 31 | | | | | 24 | 2 88 | 40 | 4 80 |
| | | | | | | | | | |
| | | | | | | | | | |
| | | | | | | | | | |
| | | | | | | | | | |

Fig. 7.9   Stock record card

## *Requisitions* (Fig. 7.10)

Strict control is kept over the issue of all requisition books, which are numbered consecutively. When a book is issued, its number and the department to which it is issued are noted. A written requisition in triplicate, signed by an authorised person, should be presented for all items issued from the stores. Details of goods and quantities required are entered on the requisition. The two top copies are sent to the stores, the third copy remaining in the book. The goods required are supplied from stock, the storeman retaining the top copy in the stores, and sending the second copy with the goods. The top copy of the requisition is used to enter the issues on the individual bin cards; it is then priced from the invoices or price lists and the value entered on the stock record cards, after which the requisition is passed to the food and beverage controller. The second copy, which is sent back to the kitchen with the goods, is used for checking the accuracy of the issues; it is then forwarded to the food and beverage control office, where it will be matched to the top copy for control purposes. For easy identification purposes the requisition books can be different colours for various departments.

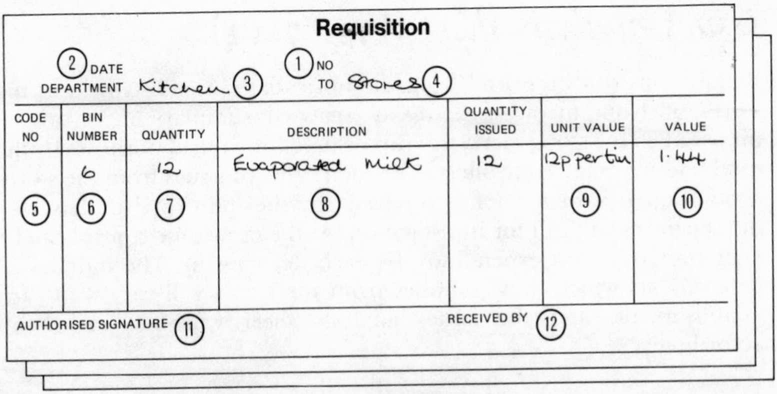

**Requisition**

(2) DATE

DEPARTMENT Kitchen (3)

(1) NO

TO Stores (4)

| CODE NO | BIN NUMBER | QUANTITY | DESCRIPTION | QUANTITY ISSUED | UNIT VALUE | VALUE |
|---|---|---|---|---|---|---|
| | 6 | 12 | Evaporated Milk | 12 | 12p per tin | 1·44 |
| (5) | (6) | (7) | (8) | | (9) | (10) |

AUTHORISED SIGNATURE (11) RECEIVED BY (12)

Fig. 7.10 Requisition (see text for explanation of numbers)
(a) Top and 2nd copy to stores. 3rd copy retained in book
(b) Top copy retained by storekeeper. 2nd copy sent back with goods
(c) Top, 2nd and 3rd copies to food and beverage controller

## *Details on requisition*

1. Requisition number (pre-printed)
2. Date
3. Department requiring goods
4. Place where goods are stored (stores, cellar, etc.)
5. Code number—this is the account code number to which the value involved will be posted
6. Bin no.—This is the bin card number from which the commodity has been booked out
7. Quantity
8. A description of the commodity including catalogue no. if any
9. Unit value—the price per unit of the commodity
10. Value—total value of goods issued
11. Authorised signature—the requisition has to be checked and signed by a person in authority, e.g. *chef de cuisine*
12. Received by—the person receiving the goods from the stores or cellar after checking the issues signs the top and second copy of the requisition.

# *Issues analysis sheet* (Fig. 7.11)

Requisitions can be priced from the up-to-date price lists held in the stores or from invoices. A weekly analysed summary sheet can be prepared by the stores clerk, this can be used for control purposes by the food and beverage controllers. The total value of issues from the stores should agree with the totals received by the individual outlets, any discrepancies will call for investigation. At the same time control can be kept over the total expenditure by each department. The number of departments which draw supplies from the stores will vary with each establishment, and the issues analysis sheet will be headed up accordingly.

Fig. 7.11  Weekly issues analysis sheet

| | | | OUTLETS | | | | | |
|---|---|---|---|---|---|---|---|---|
| DATE | REQUISITION NUMBER | VALUE £ p | KITCHEN | GRILL ROOM | STILL ROOM | FLOOR SERVICE | RESTAURANT | BANQUETING |
| | | | | | | | | |
| TOTALS | | | | | | | | |

**Weekly Issues Analysis Sheet**

# *Weekly invoice analysis sheet* (Fig. 7.12)

All invoices received into the stores should be checked and married to the order copy and delivery notes; they should then be listed and entered in the analysis columns. At the end of the week the summary is cross-cast and totalled. By this method not only is there control on expenditure, but a watchful eye can be kept on the amount spent on each type of commodity.

## Weekly Invoice Analysis Sheet

| DATE | SUPPLIER | OUR ORDER NUMBER | INVOICE | TOTAL | MEAT GAME POULTRY BACON | FISH | FATS CHEESE | EGGS | TEA & COFFEE | TINNED GOODS | NON PERISHABLES |
|------|----------|------------------|---------|-------|-------------------------|------|-------------|------|--------------|--------------|-----------------|
|  |  |  |  |  |  |  |  |  |  |  |  |
|  |  |  |  |  |  |  |  |  |  |  |  |
|  |  |  |  |  |  |  |  |  |  |  |  |
| **TOTAL** |  |  |  |  |  |  |  |  |  |  |  |
| **CREDIT NOTES** |  |  |  |  |  |  |  |  |  |  |  |
| **TOTAL** |  |  |  |  |  |  |  |  |  |  |  |

Fig. 7.12   Weekly invoice analysis sheet

# Stock checks

Regular spot checks should be made on the goods held in stock; this means that a few items daily should be physically counted and checked against the balance on the bin card. This spot checking should be planned so that all major items have been checked at least once during an accounting period, e.g. six months or one year. In addition to spot checks, food and beverage controllers should make surprise stock checks, and no prior notice should be given to the storekeeper or his staff on these occasions. Any discrepancies noted should be notified immediately to the management and corrective action taken.

## Stock Lists

| (1) BIN NUMBER | (2) DESCRIPTION OF ITEM | (3) UNIT | (4) QUANTITY | (5) UNIT PRICE | (6) TOTAL VALUE | (7) WHEN LAST CHECKED | (8) + OR − DISCREPANCY | (9) REMARKS |
|------|----------------|------|----------|------------|-------------|-----------------|----------------------|---------|
| 1 | Lemon Curd | 3·5 Kg |  |  |  |  |  |  |
| 2 | Apricot Puree | 1·5 Kg |  |  |  |  |  |  |
| 3 | almond Essence | bot. |  |  |  |  |  |  |

Fig. 7.13   Stock lists (see text for explanation of numbers)

99

# Stock lists (Fig. 7.13)

Stocktaking should be done at least once a month. Stock sheets listing all commodities held in stock are usually printed, so that it is a simple procedure to fill in the balance of each commodity at a certain date. From the stock sheets, the total capital invested in stock can be ascertained, also the rate of turnover of stock and stock levels of all commodities. Details on the stock lists (Fig. 7.13) are:

1. Bin number
2. Item
3. Unit in which stocked
4. Quantity—no. of units in stock
5. Unit price
6. Total value of stock—column (4) × column (5)
7. Date of last stock check
8. Difference (if any) between figure in column (4) and that on stock record card
9. Any comments regarding state of stock such as damage, deterioration, etc.

# Notification of price changes (Fig. 7.14)

In order that control is exercised at all times over the food cost percentages, the *chef de cuisine* and food and beverage controllers must be advised of the prices of commodities and notified of all fluctuations; this will enable them to plan menus with current prices of the ingredients in mind.

| NOTIFICATION OF PRICE CHANGES | | | | | |
|---|---|---|---|---|---|
| Item | Price on 30.4.7 | Price on 14.5.7 | | | |
| Tomatoes | £3.22 box | £4.50 box | up | | |
| Grapefruit | 12p each | 9p each | down | | |
| Cauliflower (Florets) | 20p per lb | 40p per kg | down | | |
| Lettuce | 12p each | 12p each | up | | |
| Whole Plaice | 16p each | 16p each | up | | |

Fig. 7.14   Notification of price changes

# Purchasing

In small establishments the *chef de cuisine* would be responsible for purchasing, but this is usually placed in the hands of an experienced purchasing agent in a larger organisation. Carelessness in specifying quantities and qualities or delivery dates of supplies or bad judgement in assessing prices or the right time to buy could be damaging to a business. A buyer for a hotel would normally have the following basic qualifications:

1. Training and experience in food and beverage departments.
2. Experience and good knowledge of the preparation of food, the seasonability of fruit and vegetables and other foods, butchering of meat, characteristics of wine, spirits, beer and minerals.
3. A knowledge of accounting procedures, and the ability to calculate speedily and accurately.
4. Administrative knowledge and the ability to communicate and negotiate with suppliers.

## *Purchasing methods*

The policy adopted by the purchasing officer will depend on the size, type and style of the establishment and the quantities and commodities involved. Among the methods that can be used are:

### 1. Contract purchasing
The establishment may enter into a contract with a supplier for the commodities to be supplied at regular intervals, usually at advantageous prices.

### 2. Periodical purchasing
The requirements are estimated and regular orders are placed, for example, on a month-to-month basis; this method will ensure stocks being kept at the required levels.

### 3. By requirement
Orders are placed as required; for perishable goods, this is on a day-to-day basis.

### 4. By the market purchasing
The buyer will have a list of requirements and will ask for quotations from the various suppliers of the commodities; he then compares prices and places firm orders when he can obtain the best prices, bearing in mind the quality of the provisions.

# Effective purchasing

To be effective, the buyer must take the following factors into consideration when purchasing.

## 1. Price

A skilful buyer will explore all possible suppliers, both locally and nationally, and purchase materials at the most economical price. He will constantly check alternative sources, and when comparing quotations will verify container sizes and unit values as they may vary considerably from supplier to supplier. Terms regarding trade discounts and payment for goods have also to be negotiated.

## 2. Quality and specification

Careful planning between the chefs, food and beverage controller and the buyers will establish the most suitable specifications for food to be purchased for the hotel or restaurant. This has a distinct bearing on portion control, costing and menu planning, and even the restaurant and kitchen staff required depend to a degree on the specification of goods to be purchased. Poor grades of fruit or vegetables can mean extra labour and unusually high wastage. Badly trimmed meat means more time spent on preparation, while pre-cut steaks which are either under or over weight will result in inaccurate costing. Fish and poultry should be ordered exactly by number and weight required; any variations in the weights will result in inaccurate portion sizes and costing. Suppliers should be given copies of the specifications as decided by the controllers in order that they know what standards are acceptable.

# Purchasing charts

When buying perishable goods it is useful to compile purchasing charts (Fig. 7.15) which will show the quantities based on 100 covers, which

Fig. 7.15   Purchasing charts

| | | Purchasing Charts | | |
|---|---|---|---|---|
| 100 COVERS | ITEM | SPECIFICATIONS | ORDER | PRICE QUOTES |
| | BEEF<br><br>Top Round<br>Bottom Round<br>Brisket<br>Prime Ribs<br>Sirloin Steaks<br>Filet Mignon | <br><br>Choice<br>Choice<br>Choice<br>(16–18 kg)<br>350 g<br>200 g | | |

can be multiplied or divided according to requirements. Quality specifications and up-to-the-minute prices can be inserted on the chart and this will assist the buyer when placing orders.

# Cost of ordering

With an effective stock control system overall costs can be reduced. From information extracted from the stock records an estimate of demand can be made, which could reduce the overall annual ordering and holding costs.

For example, it must be remembered that every time an order is placed it involves:

1. Telephone costs to make enquiries and obtain quotations
2. The paperwork involved in placing orders
3. The documentation of stock when goods are received
4. Accounting for purchases
5. Time and labour involved in receiving, binning and counting
6. Possibly a delivery charge by the supplier.

To estimate the cost of placing one single order one could add up the annual costs of the above and divide by the number of orders placed in a year, e.g.:

|                        |     | £   |
| ---------------------- | --- | --- |
| Stationery used        |     | 120 |
| Telephone time         |     | 200 |
| Postage                |     | 135 |
| Accounting documents   |     | 50  |
| Office Sundries        |     | 35  |
|                        |     | £540 |

| Number of orders placed | 600 |
| ----------------------- | --- |
| Cost per order          | £540 |

$$\frac{£540}{600} = 90\text{p per order}$$

Bearing in mind the estimated cost of placing one single order, by studying the usage of various items it is possible to forecast to a degree the requirements, and to place orders in a more economical manner.

# Cost of holding stock

Goods held in stock represent a capital investment which is lying dormant. If capital is invested in the normal course of business, one would expect the percentage return to be higher than what can be obtained by placing the money in the bank or other safe investment. Since stock often lies idle and produces no return, the cost of holding stock must be taken into consideration.

To estimate the cost of holding stock one would take into consideration the costs which vary proportionately with the value of stock such as:

1. Capital tied up in stock
2. Insurance costs
3. Estimated percentage loss caused by deterioration or wastage
4. Any interest charges.

To measure the effective use of capital is to express the profit earned as a percentage of the capital employed:

*Example 1:*

$$\frac{\text{Net profit}}{\text{Capital invested}} = \frac{£19,200}{£120,000} = 16\%$$

Unearned profit due to capital invested in stock, plus an estimated 1% due to loss and deterioration, and 3% of the value of stock throughout the year for insurances and other charges, will make the cost of holding stock in this case approximately 20% of the average value of the stock.

When stock is being controlled the ordering procedure must be carefully considered for, if ordering costs are minimised by a reduction in the number of orders placed, it may mean that larger quantities of materials may have to be held in stock, thus increasing the cost of holding stock; therefore the buyer must strike a careful balance between the ordering and holding costs.

# Stock valuation

Stock in hand has to be valued periodically for accounting purposes and it is a fundamental principle that stock is valued at cost price or at current market price, whichever is the lower. In order to value the stock on hand it is necessary to list each item and the cost price per unit from the invoices or price lists on a stock sheet and then value the stock. As prices can fluctuate, any *increase* in the unit price of stocks held should be disregarded until they are sold, as the value may fall again. If the present value is *lower* than the price paid, the lower value must be used when stocktaking. Some organisations prefer to value stock in hand by calculating an average price for each item over the accounting period, while others value stock at the cost of replacements, but these methods could result in undervaluing or overvaluing the stock. It is important, however, that whatever method is used it is applied consistently throughout.

# Discounts

## Trade discount

Suppliers normally provide catalogues and price lists from which their customers may order the commodities they require. As the type of customer and the quantities they order can vary considerably, prices in the catalogues are usually based on the price at which the retailer will sell to the public. In order that the retailer may make a profit, and to avoid costly reprinting of the catalogue whenever prices fluctuate, an allowance at a stated percentage is given by the manufacturer or wholesaler to the retailer; this allowance is known as trade discount and the percentage will depend on the quantities ordered by the purchaser and what is customary in 'the trade'. The items purchased are invoiced at list price less trade discount:

*Example 2:*
   List price £2·30

|  | £ |
|---|---|
| 6 cases of Pears @ £2·30 per case | 13·80 |
| *Less* 25% Trade discount | 3·45 |
| Amount to be paid: | £10·35 |

## Cash discount

To encourage prompt payment by their customers the suppliers will sometimes offer a specific percentage discount if the purchaser settles his account within a certain period of time, e.g. $2\frac{1}{4}$% discount on monthly credit account, plus $1\frac{1}{4}$% extra discount for prompt cash, which means payment within ten days of the date of the invoice. This cash discount may only be taken if the purchaser pays his account within the stated time, and can be considered as an additional percentage gross profit if taken:

*Example 3:*

|  | £ |
|---|---|
| Net amount of invoice | 10·35 |
| *Less* $2\frac{1}{2}$% cash discount | 0·26 |
| Amount due if paid promptly: | £10·09 |

# Progress test questions

1. What is the basis of a good stock control system?

2. What information should a good stock control system provide?

3. Itemise briefly the basic duties and responsibilities that have to be carried out by the storekeeper.

4. Explain the systems for ordering perishable and non-perishable goods.

5. What is the purpose of the following documents?
   (a) A delivery note
   (b) An invoice
   (c) A credit note
   (d) A statement.

6. Illustrating your answers with a diagram, describe the details and purpose of the following:
   (a) a bin card
   (b) a stock record card
   (c) a requisition
   (d) a goods received book.

7. Explain the basic procedures for stock checks in the stores.

8. What would you consider to be the essential qualities necessary for a purchasing agent to a large organisation?

9. Explain four different methods of purchasing that a buyer could use, when purchasing for a large hotel.

10. For effective purchasing a buyer must consider certain factors. Explain these factors.

11. What do you understand by the following?
    (a) Ordering costs
    (b) Cost of handling

12. Explain different methods of valuing stock in hand.

13. Explain clearly what you understand by the terms 'trade discount' and 'cash discount'.

14. Calculate the amounts due to be paid on the following accounts:

| | Total of account £ | Trade discount | Cash discount | Amount to be paid £ |
|---|---|---|---|---|
| 1. | 42·80 | 25% | 5% | |
| 2. | 120·00 | 33⅓% | 2½% | |
| 3. | 232·40 | 10% | 2½% | |
| 4. | 37·20 | 16⅔% | 5% | |
| 5. | 87·80 | 15% | 2½% | |

# CHAPTER 8

# Kitchen Control

## Duties of the *chef de cuisine*

The head chef or *chef de cuisine* in any establishment has the overall responsibility for the organisation, productiveness and efficiency of the kitchen. The larger the establishment the wider the scope and the more administrative the role becomes, but in the main the head chef has responsibility for:

1. Menu planning
2. Engaging kitchen staff
3. Kitchen organisation and delegation of duties to the staff
4. Providing management with full information on the efficiency of the kitchen operation
5. Ensuring that the required kitchen profit target is attained
6. Advising management on kitchen equipment requirements
7. Overall supervision of the kitchen, especially at service time.

## 1. *Menu planning*

The *chef de cuisine* has the opportunity to demonstrate his knowledge, skill, ingenuity and culinary art when planning menus. Not only does he have to bear in mind the basic fundamentals such as the overall balance and appeal of the menu to be offered, he must also be conscious of the cost of each item to be served if the required kitchen profit target is to be achieved. By compiling a recipe manual of all the range of dishes that are suitable for the particular establishment and keeping the unit cost cards up to date, it should be possible to offer a menu which will be not only attractive to the customers but also produce the required gross profit margin.

## 2. *Engaging kitchen staff*

The head chef as a departmental head has the responsibility of engaging staff to meet the requirements of the kitchen. From experience he will establish the number of staff necessary to carry out the various tasks, based on the type of menus to be offered and the estimated number of meals to be served. The *chef de cuisine* also has the added responsibility of keeping the labour costs for the kitchen within the percentage target set by management. This target is arrived at by the study of labour cost figures over varying periods of time and thereby establishing the average labour cost for the future comparative periods, taking any likely wage increases into consideration. A weekly labour cost statement is usually prepared showing the hourly rates, the number of hours and the amount of overtime worked by each member of staff and the total labour cost for each week. By this means the management can exercise control over labour costs for the kitchen and any unusual variances from the target percentage can be investigated and corrective action taken if necessary.

## 3. *Kitchen organisation*

Kitchen organisation means the arrangement of staff and the allocation of duties so that all the sections integrate and work as one in the kitchen, whether it is a large organisation employing over a hundred kitchen staff or a small restaurant employing only a few, a well organised kitchen will function efficiently and consequently should achieve profitability.

The head chef has responsibility for:

(a) the delegation of duties and fixing the responsibility of the individual *parties*;
(b) seeing that first-class standards of hygiene both with personnel and in the kitchen are maintained;
(c) ensuring that all staff are instructed in specifications, standards and portion control.

## 4. *Management information*

As an administrator the *chef de cuisine* has responsibility for keeping management informed on the efficiency of the kitchen operation. Various catering returns and statistical data have to be provided for management so that they may assess the profitability of the kitchen and from this budget and forecast for future operations.

## 5. *Kitchen profit*

By a careful study of the basic elements of cost, management are able to assess the minimum kitchen profit necessary to cover their labour costs and overheads and provide a reasonable net profit. For example, if a kitchen profit of 65% of turnover is required, this means the Food Cost must not exceed 35% of the turnover.

*Example 1:*

$$Sales - Food\ cost = Kitchen\ profit$$

| 100% | 35% | 65% |
|------|-----|------|
| £2,000 | £700 | £1,300 |

If the *chef de cuisine* is to keep to the required target of 35%, the value of the commodities used for the food production from the kitchen for that period should not exceed £700. In most establishments a weekly catering return is produced by the head chef showing the kitchen profit percentage; if it varies from the set target percentage, then the chef is able to take corrective action by investigating possible causes such as excessive wastage, pilfering, bad portion control, fluctuation in the prices of commodities, or by revising the menus so that the food cost percentage is adjusted for the following period.

# 6. *Kitchen equipment*

Kitchen equipment is an asset of the business and considerable capital is invested therein; it must therefore be a responsibility of the head chef to see that staff are instructed as to the correct care and use of such equipment, and that repairs and replacements are speedily dealt with so that the kitchen operation is not interrupted by any malfunction of equipment. The chef should also keep himself informed of all the latest improvements and developments and be able to recommend to management whether or not capital investment on any new kitchen equipment is justified and will improve the efficiency of the operation.

# 7. *Service time*

The purpose of production in the kitchen is to satisfy customers' wants, and all activities that lead to customer satisfaction are productive. The culmination of such production in the kitchen reaches certain peaks during the day such as breakfast, lunch and dinner times. The *chef de cuisine* has the responsibility of seeing that production flows smoothly and that peak periods are reached with the minimum amount of fuss and aggravation; the result is that money and goodwill will flow from satisfied customers, and the kitchen brigade will enjoy job satisfaction. The chef has the added responsibility of seeing that the food production for each peak period is reconciled with the sales return for that period; in other words all issues from the kitchen should result in the sale of those issues at a given profit, either as cash in the till or as a charge on a customer's account.

# Kitchen percentages

From the planned menus the chef is able to calculate the quantities required for food production and requisition the commodities needed. Strict control must be exercised over all receipts into the kitchen, for they are stock that must be accounted for in a financial return. Perishable goods are usually received direct into the kitchen, the delivery note being signed as correct by an authorised member of the kitchen staff; it is then entered into the analysed kitchen day book. The delivery note and following invoice are then passed to the food and beverage controller and thereafter to the accounts department. Any dry goods from stores or requirements from the cellar are obtained by completing the official requisition form in triplicate. Goods received from the stores or cellar should be checked against the copy requisition when they are received into the kitchen. These will also be entered into the analysed kitchen day book.

## *Kitchen day book* (Fig. 8.1)

This book can be maintained in pad form with several copies for distribution to the various control departments or in an analysed loose leaf form. The purpose of this book is to record and analyse all receivals into the kitchen. From this analysis it is possible for the head chef to know exactly how much is spent on each type of commodity, and what percentage of the total weekly receivals it represents—any deviances from the normal percentage spent on any particular commodity will alert the chef and call for investigation. A record of the total receivals into the kitchen will enable the chef to keep control over his kitchen profit. When completing the summary of this analysis any opening stock must be added to the receivals and closing stock deducted to arrive at the actual cost of food consumed.

# Staff meals

If the terms of employment necessitate employees living in, then their meals are usually free and considered as a benefit in kind. However, the cost of feeding staff is usually included in the cost of food consumed when in fact it is part of the cost of employing labour. Therefore in order to arrive at the true kitchen profit, the cost of staff meals must be deducted from the total food cost and transferred to the labour cost.

Some caterers calculate an average allowance per person per day for meals taken during the normal course of duty. A more accurate method is for each employee to record the meals taken on their weekly time sheet, and the wages clerk values the cost of meals from the unit costing or menu costing cards (see Part 1, Chapter 2.)

# Kitchen Day Book

WEEK ENDING 7 June 19 - -

| DATE | SUPPLIER | DELIVERY NOTE REC. NO. | TOTAL | MEAT | POULTRY | FISH | GROCERY | GREEN GROCERY | MILK | BREAD | ICE CREAM | DRY GOODS | WINES & SPIRITS |
|---|---|---|---|---|---|---|---|---|---|---|---|---|---|
| June 1 | Jones Bros. | Inv. 23 | 180.00 | 150.00 | 30.00 | | | | | | | | |
| 1 | Atlas Bakery | Inv. 36 | 7.00 | | | | | | | 7.00 | | | |
| 1 | Stores | Rec. 10 | 26.00 | | | | | | | | | 26.00 | |
| 1 | Brook Dairy | Inv. 66 | 4.00 | | | | | | 4.00 | | | | |
| 1 | Cellar | Rec. 11 | 3.50 | | | | | | | | | | 3.50 |
| 2 | Challans | Inv. 112 | 55.00 | | | 55.00 | | | | | | | |
| 2 | Dunn & Co | Inv. 32 | 40.00 | | | | | 40.00 | | | | | |
| 3 | Jones & Co | Inv. 36 | 100.00 | 100.00 | | | | | | | | | |
| 3 | Atlas Bakery | Inv. 72 | 4.00 | | | | | | | 4.00 | | | |
| 3 | Brook Dairy | Inv. 84 | 3.00 | | | | | | 3.00 | | | | |
| 3 | A. B. Howson | Inv. 312 | 35.00 | | | | 35.00 | | | | | | |
| 3 | Stores | Rec. 12 | 40.50 | | | | | | | | | 40.50 | |
| 4 | Jones Bros. | Inv. 38 | 105.00 | 65.00 | 40.00 | | | | | | | | |
| 5 | Atlas Bakery | Inv. 81 | 3.00 | | | | | | | 3.00 | | | |
| 5 | Challans | Inv. 133 | 50.00 | | | 50.00 | | | | | | | |
| 5 | Dunn & Co. | Inv. 47 | 44.00 | | | | | 44.00 | | | | | |
| | TOTAL | | 700.00 | 315.00 | 70.00 | 105.00 | 35.00 | 84.00 | 7.00 | 14.00 | | 66.50 | 3.50 |
| | % OF TOTAL | | 100% | 45% | 10% | 15% | 5% | 12% | 1% | 2% | | 9.5% | 5% |

SUMMARY

| | |
|---|---|
| OPENING STOCK | £15.00 |
| ADD MONEY RECEIVED | £700.00 |
| | £715.00 |
| CLOSING STOCK | £10.00 |
| COST OF FOOD CONSUMED | £705.00 |

| | | |
|---|---|---|
| SALES | £2000.00 | 100% |
| LESS COST OF FOOD CONSUMED | £705.00 | 35.25% |
| KITCHEN PROFIT | £1295.00 | 64.75% |

Fig. 8.1  Kitchen day book

# Effects of staff meals on kitchen percentages

The following examples will illustrate how kitchen percentages are distorted if the cost of feeding staff is included in the cost of food consumed, in particular when establishments have a positive seasonable business and carry a permanent staff during the off season. In such cases the cost of staff meals could exceed the cost of food sold and would result in a complete distortion of the actual kitchen profit.

*Example 2:*

### Kitchen Profit Statement
### for week ending 7 June

|  | £ | £ | % |
|---|---|---|---|
| Food sales |  | 2,000 | 100·00 |
| Food cost: |  |  |  |
| Opening stock 1.6.19.. | 15 |  |  |
| *Add* Receivals into kitchen | 700 |  |  |
|  | 715 |  |  |
| *Less* Closing stock 7.6.19.. | 10 |  |  |
| Cost of food consumed |  | 705 | 35·25 |
| Kitchen profit |  | £1,295 | 64·75 |

If the cost of staff meals for the week amounted to £55, note the effect on the kitchen profit and the percentages if the cost of feeding the staff is deducted from the cost of food consumed.

### Kitchen Profit Statement
### for week ending 7 June

|  | £ | £ | % |
|---|---|---|---|
| Food sales |  | 2,000 | 100·00 |
| Food cost: |  |  |  |
| Opening stock 1.6.19.. | 15 |  |  |
| *Add* Receivals into kitchen | 700 |  |  |
|  | 715 |  |  |
| *Less* Closing stock 7.6.19.. | 10 |  |  |
| Cost of food consumed | 705 |  |  |
| *Less* Cost of staff meals | 55 |  |  |
|  |  | 650 | 32·50 |
| Kitchen profit |  | £1,350 | 67·50 |

It must be remembered when fixing kitchen profit targets that it should be clearly defined whether the percentage is inclusive or exclusive of staff meals. A watchful eye should also be kept on what percentage of the total food cost is attributable to the feeding of staff.

# Control of issues

The most simple method of controlling issues from the kitchen is by the triple checking system. Each waiter is issued with a numbered waiter's check pad. These are in triplicate. The top copy is handed into the kitchen for the order required, the second copy goes to the cashier to make out the customer's bill, and the third copy is retained by the waiter for his reference. At the end of service all three copies are eventually married together, cross-checked and analysed by the food and beverage controllers. The waiters' check pads are designed to meet the requirements of each particular establishment. The first and main course can be ordered on the first check followed by another check for the sweet course and handed into the kitchen as required (Fig. 8.2), or a check pad

Fig. 8.2   Waiter's food check

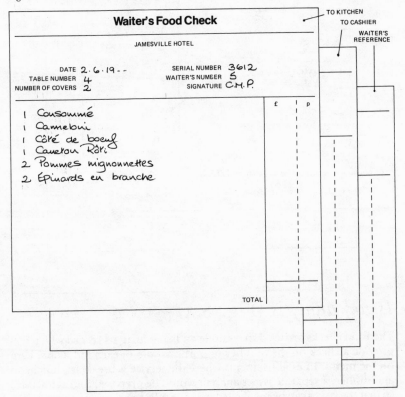

with the top copy in perforated slips which are torn off for each course. The second and waiter's copies show the complete order intact. For control purposes the food check should show:

1. The serial number of the food check
2. The date
3. The waiter's number
4. Table no.
5. No. of covers
6. The order
7. The waiter's signature or initials.

Fig. 8.3   Waiter's perforated food check

| Waiter's Food Check | | £ | p | | |
|---|---|---|---|---|---|
| 0281 | 2 Shrimp Cocktail | 4 | | | TO KITCHEN |
| 0281 | 2 Cream of Chicken | 4 | | | TO CASHIER |
| 0281 | 1 Roast Lamb  1 Roast Duck | 4 | | | WAITER'S REFERENCE |
| 0281 | 2 Peas  2 Pots | 4 | | | |
| 0281 | 1 Apple Crumble  1 Fruit Salad | 4 | | | |
| 0281 | 2 Coffee | 4 | | | |
| 0281 | | TOTAL | | | |

TABLE NUMBER **6**    SERIAL NUMBER **2234**    DATE **7.6.19..**
NO. OF COVERS **2**    WAITER'S NUMBER **4**    SIGNATURE **G.u.P.**

# Issues analysis (Fig. 8.4)

The food checks are used to compile an issues analysis record which will provide a check on the number of portions sold of each individual item on the menu. In establishments where the service is breakfast, luncheon and dinner, a separate issues analysis would be prepared for each service so that the issues can be reconciled with the bills or charges to the guest. In self-service or continuous service restaurants one issues analysis sheet would list all items offered on the menu.

At the end of service the food checks handed into the kitchen are sorted

Fig. 8.4    Issues analysis

## Issues Analysis Sheet

SERVICE: DINNER

DATE  15. 8. 19. _ _

MENU NUMBER

| TABLE NUMBER | NUMBER OF COVERS | WAITER NUMBER | FOOD CHECK NUMBER | MENU ANALYSIS | | | | | | | | | | | | | | | | | | | | | | BILL NUMBER | SALES TOTAL |
|---|---|---|---|---|---|---|---|---|---|---|---|---|---|---|---|---|---|---|---|---|---|---|---|---|---|---|---|
| | | | | 1 | 2 | 3 | 4 | 5 | 6 | 7 | 8 | 9 | 10 | 11 | 12 | 13 | 14 | 15 | 16 | 17 | 18 | 19 | 20 | 21 | 22 | | |
| 1 | 4 | 17 | 0236 | 2 | 1 | 1 | 3 | 1 | 1 | 2 | 1 | 4 | 2 | | 1 | 1 | 3 | 1 | | | 2 | | | | | | | |
| 2 | 2 | 6 | 0144 | 2 | | | | 2 | | 1 | 1 | 1 | 1 | | 2 | | | | 2 | | 2 | | | | | | | |
| 3 | | | | | | | | | | | | | | | | | | | | | | | | | | | | |
| 4 | | | | | | | | | | | | | | | | | | | | | | | | | | | | |
| 5 | | | | | | | | | | | | | | | | | | | | | | | | | | | | |
| 6 | | | | | | | | | | | | | | | | | | | | | | | | | | | | |
| 7 | | | | | | | | | | | | | | | | | | | | | | | | | | | | |
| 8 | | | | | | | | | | | | | | | | | | | | | | | | | | | | |
| 9 | | | | | | | | | | | | | | | | | | | | | | | | | | | | |
| 10. | | | | | | | | | | | | | | | | | | | | | | | | | | | | |
| 11 | | | | | | | | | | | | | | | | | | | | | | | | | | | | |
| 12 | | | | | | | | | | | | | | | | | | | | | | | | | | | | |
| 13 | | | | | | | | | | | | | | | | | | | | | | | | | | | | |
| 14 | | | | | | | | | | | | | | | | | | | | | | | | | | | | |
| | | | TOTALS | | | | | | | | | | | | | | | | | | | | | | | | | |

ANALYSIS

FOOD COST OF PORTIONS SOLD  £                                    KITCHEN PROFIT (    %) £

PLUS PRE-PORTIONED BUTTER, SAUCES SUNDRIES ETC  £              TOTAL SALES (100%) £

TOTAL FOOD COST (    %)  £                    LABOUR COST (% OF SALES)  £

into table numbers and each check is analysed (Fig. 8.4). The total number of portions served plus any remaining in the kitchen should reconcile with the number produced. This information will also provide the *chef de cuisine* with a guide as to:

1. Which items on the menu have proved to be the most popular
2. The average number of covers to be catered for
3. What production is necessary to cover demand
4. The percentage of wastage and how it can be avoided
5. Labour requirements to meet production
6. Any menu changes necessary
7. The food cost for the number of portions sold compared with the actual cost of receivals into the kitchen.

By entering the value of food sales from each bill, arriving at a total food sales figure and deducting the total food cost of portions sold, a further check can be made on kitchen profit.

## Issues analysis sheet

If the menu is a simple 3-course table d'hôte, the menu should be given a number to be written on the issues analysis sheet, but in a comprehensive à la carte menu each item would be given a number.

| *Example 3:* | *Menu—Dinner* | *Item no.* |
|---|---|---|
| Appetisers | Tomato juice | 1 |
| | Melon cocktail | 2 |
| | Pâté de foie-gras | 3 |
| Soups | Consommé belle fermière | 4 |
| | Crème Malakoff | 5 |
| Main Course | Boiled turbot, shrimp sauce | 6 |
| | Roast chicken with bread sauce | 7 |
| | Roast quarter of lamb boulangère, mint sauce | 8 |
| Vegetables | Whole green beans | 9 |
| | Buttered broccoli | 10 |
| Potatoes | Roast | 11 |
| | Boiled | 12 |
| | Creamed | 13 |
| Sweets | Charlotte normande | 14 |
| | Lemon ice cream | 15 |
| | Sweets from trolley | 16 |
| | Cheeseboard | 17 |
| | After-dinner mints | 18 |
| | Coffee | 19 |

# Control of trolleys

When cold buffet tables, hot joints or sweet trolleys are stocked for the restaurant, strict issues control must be operated. The kitchen will record on a consumption sheet (Fig. 8.5) exactly what is issued to each cold table, hotplate or trolley and the estimated portion yield from each item.

Customers can be served direct from the trolleys by the waiters or waitresses or a senior member of the restaurant staff will supervise the issues from the trolleys, the waiter only being supplied by exchanging a food check for the portion required. When the trolleys are returned to the kitchen the number of portions left are counted and entered on the consumption return. The stock at the start less returns should equal the number of portions consumed; any discrepancies should be investigated. The total portions consumed of each item can be transferred to the master issues analysis sheet included in the total food cost and reconciled with portions charged to the customer.

Fig. 8.5  Consumption sheet

| ITEM | ISSUED | PORTION YIELD | PORTIONS RETURNED | PORTIONS CONSUMED | PORTIONS SOLD AS PER CHECK | SALES £ p | DISCREPANCY + | DISCREPANCY − |
|------|--------|---------------|-------------------|-------------------|---------------------------|-----------|---------------|---------------|
| Creme Caramel | 12 | 12 | 4 | 8 | 7 | 2.45 | | −1 |
| Barais Rubane | 2 | 12 | 6 | 6 | 6 | 3.90 | − | − |
| Lemon meraingue Pie | 2 | 16 | − | 16 | 14 | 10.50 | | −2 |
| Savarin | 2 | 16 | 4 | 12 | 14 | 13.30 | − | − |

**Sweet Trolley** — DATE 7.6.19--  STATION 2  SERVICE Dinner

# Pre-portioned sundries

Any pre-portioned sundries such as butter served as accompaniments to the meal, if issued from the kitchen, must be strictly accounted for. The total value of these issues is added to the food cost on the issues analysis sheet.

# Menu counts (Fig. 8.6)

Regular menu count checks will highlight the most popular items and also serve as a check to control wastage.

| DINNER ITEM | NUMBER OF COVERS | % OF TOTAL COVERS | PORTION YIELD | AMOUNT ORDERED | AMOUNT USED | AMOUNT LEFT | CHECKED |
|---|---|---|---|---|---|---|---|
| | | | **Menu Count** | | | | |
| Duck | 38 | 34.5 | 4 portion product | 12 | 10 | 2 | |
| Sirloin | 60 | 54.5 | 10 to ½ strip | 7 strips | 6 | 1 strip | |
| Trout | 12 | 11.0 | 1 | 20 | 12 | 8 | |
| TOTAL COVERS | 110 | 100.00% | | | | | |

DATE 7·6·19 —
MENU NUMBER 21

Fig. 8.6   Menu count

# Centralised production kitchens

In large-scale operations, where there is a centralised production unit distributing to several different retail outlets as opposed to a kitchen geared towards food service for a hotel or restaurant, control must be exercised over the whole production operation and over supplies to each of the individual units. By analysing the food sales of the separate units, forecasts of demand can be made and production targets set. Commodities required for production are ordered as per targets set. With the increasing use of frozen foods wastage can also be much reduced. Total receivals into the production unit are redistributed to the various production centres, e.g. to the kitchen, pastry and frozen food sections. Each section can be controlled by reconciling the cost of receivals with the cost of goods distributed to the retail outlets, and overall control can be exercised by reconciling total food consumption with total distribution. If the labour cost for each section is isolated, then the productivity and efficiency of each section can be assessed.

*Example 4:*

A large production unit supplies three different types of restaurants in the same building, Units 1, 2, 3, and 2 other small outlets, Units 4 and 5. It has a main kitchen with a pastry section and frozen food production unit. The following documents (Figs. 8.7–9) illustrate a simple system for controlling the operation if all figures are at cost. The trading results from each individual unit can be assessed and an overall trading result can be obtained by collating the figures.

Fig. 8.7   Centralised production: frozen food unit weekly analysis

Fig. 8.8   Centralised production: pastry section weekly analysis

## Frozen Food Production

WEEK ENDING

| STOCK RECEIVED | £ | p | DISTRIBUTION (AT COST) | £ | p |
|---|---|---|---|---|---|
| DEBIT | | | CREDIT TO | | |
| OPENING STOCK | | | UNIT 1 | | |
| DRY GOODS | | | UNIT 2 | | |
| PERISHABLES | | | UNIT 3 | | |
| PASTRY | | | UNIT 4 | | |
| WINES | | | UNIT 5 | | |
| DISPOSABLES | | | | | |
| | | | SUB TOTAL | | |
| | | | *PLUS* CLOSING STOCK | | |
| TOTAL | | | TOTAL | | |
| PRODUCTION TARGET £<br>PRODUCTION ACTUAL £ | | | LABOUR COST £ | | |

## Pastry Food Production

WEEK ENDING

| STOCK RECEIVED | £ | p | DISTRIBUTION (AT COST) | £ | p |
|---|---|---|---|---|---|
| DEBIT | | | CREDIT TO | | |
| OPENING STOCK | | | UNIT 1 | | |
| DRY GOODS | | | UNIT 2 | | |
| PERISHABLES | | | UNIT 3 | | |
| WINES | | | UNIT 4 | | |
| DISPOSABLES | | | UNIT 5 | | |
| | | | FROZEN FOOD SECTION | | |
| | | | SUB TOTAL | | |
| | | | *PLUS* CLOSING STOCK | | |
| TOTAL | | | TOTAL | | |
| PRODUCTION TARGET £<br>PRODUCTION ACTUAL £ | | | LABOUR COST £ | | |

## Production Unit Summary Sheet

WEEK ENDING

| STOCK RECEIVED | £ | p | DISTRIBUTION | ANALYSIS | | | |
| --- | --- | --- | --- | --- | --- | --- | --- |
| | | | | MAIN KITCHEN | FROZEN FOOD | PASTRY | TOTAL |
| OPENING STOCK | | | UNIT 1 | | | | |
| DRY GOODS | | | UNIT 2 | | | | |
| PERISHABLES | | | UNIT 3 | | | | |
| PASTRY | | | UNIT 4 | | | | |
| WINES | | | UNIT 5 | | | | |
| DISPOSABLES | | | | | | | |
| TOTAL CONSUMPTION | | | TOTAL DISTRIBUTION | | | | |

Fig. 8.9  Centralised production weekly summary

## Retail unit control

A weekly summary sheet prepared by each unit will show food consumption and can be reconciled with the issues analysis from the main production unit. As the unit will undoubtedly have receivals from other sources, such as wines and spirits, cigarettes and tobacco, and small items for counter sales, a complete analysis is necessary to assess the profitability of the unit.

# Catering results

The head chef or kitchen supervisor will need a record of results each week to measure the success of the operation, especially if a kitchen profit percentage target has been set. The total food sales figures for the week are obtained from the analysed sales summary sheets prepared by the cashiers or food and beverage controllers, and the cost of food consumed

## Unit Control Summary Sheet

WEEK ENDING                                                                 GOODS RECEIVED

|  | KITCHEN | DRY GOODS | PASTRY | FROZEN FOOD | TOTAL | DISPOSABLES | COUNTER SALES | CIGARETTES & TOBACCO | WINES & SPIRITS | TOTAL |
|---|---|---|---|---|---|---|---|---|---|---|
| MON | | | | | | | | | | |
| TUES | | | | | | | | | | |
| WED | | | | | | | | | | |
| THURS | | | | | | | | | | |
| FRI | | | | | | | | | | |
| SAT | | | | | | | | | | |
| SUN | | | | | | | | | | |
| TOTALS | | | | | | | | | | |

| FOOD CONSUMPTION | £ | p | | DISPOSABLES | COUNTER SALES | CIGARETTES & TOBACCO | WINES & SPIRITS | TOTAL |
|---|---|---|---|---|---|---|---|---|
| OPENING STOCK | | | OPENING STOCK | | | | | |
| TOTAL PERISHABLES RECEIVED | | | TOTAL RECEIVED | | | | | |
| TOTAL DRY GOODS RECEIVED TRANSFERS IN | | | TRANSFERS IN | | | | | |
| SUB TOTAL | | | SUB TOTAL | | | | | |
| TRANSFER OUT | | | TRANSFERS OUT | | | | | |
| SUB TOTAL | | | SUP TOTAL | | | | | |
| LESS CLOSING STOCK | | | LESS CLOSING STOCK | | | | | |
| TOTAL FOOD CONSUMPTION | | | TOTAL | | | | | |

Fig. 8.10   Retail unit control summary

less staff meals will provide the cost of total food sold. From this information a simple cumulative percentage record can be prepared. The chef can then note any deviations from target and take action if appropriate.

Fig. 8.11   Cumulative results sheet

## Accumulative Catering Result

KITCHEN PROFIT TARGET  65%

| WEEK ENDING | TOTAL SALES | | COST OF FOOD SOLD | | KITCHEN PROFIT | | THIS WEEK | | TO DATE | |
|---|---|---|---|---|---|---|---|---|---|---|
| | THIS WEEK | TO DATE | THIS WEEK | TO DATE | THIS WEEK | TO DATE | % | + − | % | + − |
| 19 – | £ p | £ p | £ p | £ p | £ p | £ p | | | | |
| Aprie 1 | 2000·00 | 2000·00 | 700·00 | 700·00 | 1300·00 | 1300·00 | 65 | 0 | 65 | 0 |
| 7 | 2100·00 | 4100·00 | 798·00 | 1498·00 | 1302·00 | 2602·00 | 62 | -3 | 63·4 | -1·5 |
| 14 | 2250·00 | 6350·00 | 810·00 | 2308·00 | 1440·00 | 4042·00 | 64 | -1 | 63·6 | -1·4 |
| 28 | 2150 00 | 8600·00 | 731·00 | 3039·00 | 1419·00 | 5461·00 | 66 | +1 | 442 | -0·8 |

# Fraud in the kitchen

There are many types of frauds perpetrated in the kitchen and only spot checks and constant vigilance on the part of the *chef de cuisine*, controllers and supervisors will combat them. It must be remembered that any misappropriation of commodities booked to the kitchen account will make it difficult to achieve the kitchen profit target, so any deviances from the required percentages should be investigated. The most common types of fraud are:

1. *Eating by staff.* Few people consider that a member of staff helping himself to food in the kitchen is technically a fraud. But if a certain number of portions to be sold at a profit are required from a certain quantity of prepared food, then by virtue of nibbling the staff are not only defrauding the management of the cost of the food but also the profit it should have yielded when sold.
2. *Pilfering.* Fruit, eggs, packaged food are items easily put in shopping bags or handbags and carried out. Locker rooms for staff should be outside the kitchen and no bags allowed inside the kitchen. Anyone attempting to carry items out on their person should be easily visible to vigilant supervisors.

## Further precautions

1. Receiving goods directly into the kitchen should be in the hands of a responsible member of staff who should check the goods carefully.
2. Goods booked from the stores or cellars on requisitions should be checked against the copy requisition in the kitchen. Quantities should be weighed and numbers checked.
3. Regular spot checks should be made on portion sizes served to customers. By serving small portions a surplus can be built up to be either eaten by staff or carried out. This practice will result in complaints from the customers and loss of goodwill.
4. Pre-portion packs such as butter, jams and sauces are easily carried out. These should be counted and a check kept on their issue.
5. No issues should be made at the hotplate without a covering waiter's food check. 'Innocents' on the hotplate are a big opportunity for unscrupulous waiting staff who obtain food without giving a check, especially at a very busy time; this can be converted into cash or eaten or used to give larger portions and thus encourage bigger tips for themselves.
6. The most difficult and costly fraud to attack is that perpetrated by the head chef or supervisor in collusion with outsiders. Goods are booked to the kitchen account and then sold at the back door to unscrupulous distributors. This type of fraud will soon be reflected in the kitchen

percentage and customer dissatisfaction in not getting value for money. Constant surveillance of all aspects of the kitchen operation is therefore necessary at all times.

# Progress test questions

1. Discuss the role and responsibilities of the *chef de cuisine* in a large organisation.

2. What is the purpose of the kitchen day book, and what useful information can it provide?

3. (a) Explain two methods of assessing the cost of staff meals.
   (b) What adjustment should be made to cost percentages in respect of staff meals?
   (c) Prepare a kitchen profit statement for the week ending 7 July 19.. from the following information:

   | | £ |
   |---|---|
   | Opening stock 1 July | 35 |
   | Cost of staff meals for week | 61 |
   | Total receivals into kitchen | 1,095 |
   | Closing stock 7 July | 25 |
   | Food sales for week ending 7 July | 2,700 |

4. Detail the information obtainable from an issues analysis, and explain in what way can it be of guidance to the *chef de cuisine*.

5. Explain what method you would use to control issues to hot joint or sweet trolleys. Illustrate your answer with a diagram of a suitable control document.

6. A large organisation has a central kitchen with a separate frozen food production unit and pastry production unit, and distributes the food produced to the following outlets: the executive staff restaurant, a waiter service restaurant, a self-service cafeteria and two other small restaurants. Describe a simple control system for the production units and the retail outlets, illustrating your answer with suitable control documents.

7. From the following information prepare an accumulative catering result statement.

The percentage target is 60%.

| 19.. | | Sales £ | Food cost £ |
|---|---|---|---|
| Mar. | 1 | 1,500 | 600 |
| | 7 | 1,580 | 632 |
| | 14 | 1,660 | 730 |
| | 21 | 1,680 | 756 |
| | 28 | 1,750 | 735 |
| Apr. | 4 | 1,800 | 774 |
| | 11 | 1,810 | 706 |
| | 18 | 1,850 | 870 |
| | 25 | 1,900 | 722 |

8. Discuss some of the frauds that are perpetrated in the kitchen and explain what steps you can take to combat them.

# CHAPTER 9

# Wines, Spirits & Beer Control

## Cost control pattern

The control pattern for wines, spirits and beers is basically the same as the food control system.

1. Orders have to be placed
2. Goods are received into the cellar and have to be recorded on the bin cards, stock record cards and in the goods received book
3. Issues are made from the cellar to the various bars and other outlets on duly authorised requisitions, and entered on the stock records
4. Sales from bars and restaurants have to be recorded
5. Purchases and sales have to be analysed.

The complexity of the stock control system will depend on the size of the establishment and the extent of the information required by management. A small hotel or restaurant would probably require only a simple stock control system which could be operated by the cellarman or a stock clerk. A large organisation would probably require comprehensive information from their control systems in order to forecast and budget for future operations. The larger the hotel or restaurant, the greater the capital investment and range of stock required, therefore the greater the necessity for supervision and stock control.

The following records and documents are those needed to provide the information. For smaller establishments the documents and records could be condensed and simplified.

## *Suppliers' record cards* (Fig. 9.1)

Details of suppliers should be maintained on a card index system either in alphabetical order of suppliers' names, or preferably in alphabetical order of the wines, spirits or beers stocked as per the wine lists. These records will provide full details of the suppliers and are ready means of recording information on orders. All price changes should be recorded on the suppliers' cards which also serve as a permanent record.

## Wine Record Card

| ADVOCAT de KUYPER | SUPPLIER | Simmonds & Sons 2 Eastgate St. London WC2 01-092 911 | | | BEAUJOLAIS (French) | SUPPLIER | R Wilson Limited 14 Down St. London EC2 01-091 1006 | |
|---|---|---|---|---|---|---|---|---|
| DATE | PRICE PER ( ) BOTTLES | PRICE PER ( ) ½ BOTTLES | PRICE PER ½ BOTTLE | | DATE | PRICE PER ( ) BOTTLE | PRICE PER ½ BOTTLE | |
| | | | | | | | | |
| | | | | | | | | |
| | | | | | | | | |

Fig. 9.1   Suppliers' record cards

# *Master wine lists* (Fig. 9.2)

Master wine lists are prepared by management, and from this, the wines, spirits and beer stock levels are decided. They will show the cost price, the selling price, and gross profit margin (percentage or cash) on each item to be carried in stock.

Fig. 9.2   Master wine list

## Master Wine List

| | | MEASURES PER BOTTLE | COST PRICE | SELLING PRICE | GROSS PROFIT % |
|---|---|---|---|---|---|
| RED WINES | Beaujolais (French) Macon (French) St. Emilion (French) Médoc (French) Châteauneuf du Pape (French) | | | | |
| WHITE WINES | Pouilly Fuissé (French) Petit Chablis (French) Sauternes (French) Liebfraumilch (German) Ruffino Orvieto (Italian) | | | | |
| | | | | | |

# Purchasing

All items to be held in stock are decided by the bar managers. The head cellarman will examine his stock regularly comparing his stock levels with the re-order level on the bin cards. Any item that is below or at re-order point will be listed on the 'list of requirements' (Fig. 9.3) which will be passed through to the purchasing agent so that official orders can be prepared.

Fig. 9.3    List of requirements for the cellar

| | **List of Requirements** | | | | |
|---|---|---|---|---|---|
| BIN NUMBER | ITEM | UNIT OF PURCHASE | CATALOGUE NUMBER | QUANTITY REQUIRED | |
| | | | | | |
| | | | | | |
| | | | | | |
| | | | | | |

## *Purchasing orders*

All orders are made out on official order forms. These are usually in sets, the number of copies depending on the requirements of the management, for example:

| Copy | | |
|---|---|---|
| 1 | (White) | To the supplier |
| 2 | (Blue) | Food and beverage controller |
| 3 | (Pink) | Accounts department |
| 4 | (Yellow) | Receiving department |
| 5 | (Green) | Purchasing |
| 6 | (White) | Head office |

## *Request to raise a purchase order* (Fig. 9.4)

As the stock carried by the hotel is based on the master wine list, when an item is required which is not normally carried in stock, a request to raise a purchase order (Fig. 9.4) should be completed. This form is usually in triplicate, the 1st and 2nd copies being passed to the general manager for his approval and signature. The person originating the request keeps Copy 3. After the request has been approved, Copy 1 goes to the purchasing agent, and Copy 2 is filed by the food and beverage controller.

| Request to Raise Purchase Order | | | NUMBER | |
| | | | DATE | |

| NAME OF SUPPLIER | QUANTITY | ITEM | VALUE PER UNIT | REASON FOR REQUEST |
|---|---|---|---|---|
| | | | | |
| | | | | |
| | | | | |
| | | | | |
| | | | | |
| | | | | |

| SIGNATURE OF PERSON REQUESTING ITEMS | SIGNATURE OF APPROVAL |
|---|---|
| DISTRIBUTION<br>COPY 1 PURCHASING AGENT<br>COPY 2 FOOD AND BEVERAGES CONTROLLER<br>COPY 3 ORIGINATOR | FOR OFFICE USE<br>DATE<br>ORDER NUMBER<br>SUPPLIER |

Fig. 9.4   Special purchase request

## Telephone orders

When the purchasing agent has received the 'list of requirements' (Fig. 9.3) and any approved 'requests to raise purchase orders' (Fig. 9.4), purchase order sets will be prepared, and to expedite delivery the purchasing agent could telephone details to the suppliers and arrange delivery dates and times. The purchase orders would then be despatched to confirm the telephoned orders.

As far as practicable it is advisable to arrange deliveries to take place after 14.00, as this will assist in the planning of staff for the cellar and receiving areas.

## Notification of price changes

As with orders for food, it is essential that the management and controllers are fully informed of any price changes on the items carried as stock, and therefore a weekly 'notification of price changes' (see Fig. 7.14) should be completed and distributed to:

The hotel manager
The bars manager
The food and beverage controller
Head cellarman

With a copy for the files in the purchasing department.

# Receiving goods

Staff should be instructed on the standard procedures for the receipt and checking of goods into the cellar as follows:

1. Copies of orders are passed to the receiving clerk, who should file them in delivery date order, attaching them to a clipboard for easy accessibility.
2. When the goods arrive they should be checked against the delivery note and the copy order. If there is no delivery note with the goods, a 'dummy delivery note' should be made out.
3. If the goods agree with the delivery note and the copy order, the receiving clerk will sign the supplier's copy delivery note as correct.
4. If goods are not as ordered, they should not be accepted unless it is only the quantity that is short, in which case both the delivery note and copy order will be amended to show the actual quantity received, and the receiving clerk will only sign for this quantity.
5. The receiving clerk must then notify the head cellarman immediately that the goods are awaiting collection from the receiving area, for until they are removed to the cellar, their safe keeping is the responsibility of the receiving clerk.
6. When they are collected by the head cellarman, he must sign the receiving clerk's copy order for what is being received, and take the supplier's delivery note.
7. Part orders received are marked off the same copy order.
8. Copy orders, and any invoices received and a control list of their numbers, are forwarded to the food and beverage controllers, usually at the end of each week.

## *Receiving goods into the cellar*

The responsibility for the goods passes from the receiving clerk to the head cellarman at the time he signs the copy order. Therefore:

1. Before signing the copy order, he should carefully check that the goods are as stated, particularly where alterations have been made to the copy order.
2. Arrangements should be made by the head cellarman to remove the goods to the cellar as quickly as possible.
3. Once the goods are in the cellar they should be checked in detail against the delivery note. The condition of the goods should be examined and if suspect the bars manager should be asked for an opinion.
4. Any discrepancies or sub-standard goods should be notified to the food and beverage controllers and purchasing agent, who have the responsibility of dealing with suppliers.

5. The delivery notes are used for writing up the bin cards (Fig. 7.8).
6. If an order is incomplete at the end of the week, the head cellarman will raise a further order for the balance if required.

## Requisitions on the cellar

Goods from the cellars should only be issued on receipt of a written requisition (Fig. 7.10) in triplicate signed by an authorised person. The food and beverage controller will supply the head cellarman with a list of approved signatures, and only those signatures on requisitions should be accepted by the cellar staff.

## Issues from the cellar

Requisitions from the bars and restaurants are usually placed in a central point in the front office and collected by the head cellarman or his deputy every morning when they collect the cellar keys.

# Cellar procedures

1. All requisitions should be carefully checked to ensure that the details are correct, and in particular that they are signed by an authorised person from the list of approved signatures.
2. The goods should be drawn from the bin, and the quantities issued entered in the 'quantity issued' column (Fig. 7.10) of all three copies of the requisition.
3. If an item is out of stock, OOS should be written in the 'quantity issued' column of the requisition, and details of this particular item should be entered immediately on the 'list of requirements' list (Fig. 9.3).
4. When the items are ready for delivery they are checked over by the porter who will deliver them to the outlets and he will sign all three copies of the requisition. Copies 1 and 2 go with the goods.
5. The 3rd copy of the requisition stays in the cellar where it is used to post the goods 'out' on the bin cards and stock record cards.
6. In certain circumstances requisitions may be received direct from the bar during the course of the day, and these will be dealt with in the same way.
7. If there is an emergency during the hours the cellar is normally closed, and the duty food and beverage controller obtains the cellar keys and issues stock, the head cellarman will check that the requisitions left have been duly completed and process them in the correct way.

# Containers

Many containers are chargeable and therefore empty containers must be collected in the receiving area by the cellar staff and the supplier notified that they are ready for collection—the receiving clerk must obtain a signature from the van driver that he has collected the empties. 'Return slips' should be passed to the food and beverage controller who will ensure that a credit for these returned containers is received by the accounts section.

# Fixed bars

The stock levels of the 'fixed bars' of a hotel are decided by the bar managers. The types of beverage stocked and the stock levels, which are known as 'pars', are agreed after a careful analysis of the bar consumption figures. The 'pars' and the varieties of beverage should not be changed without the prior approval of the bar managers. Each bar should have a coded list of items to be stocked and towards the close of business each day the head barman should examine his stock and make out his requisitions for the following day based on the day's consumption, and these requisitions should bring his stock level up to 'par'.

The requisition in triplicate will be placed in the special box provided in the front office to be collected by the head cellarman the following morning.

If a fixed bar runs out of stock during the course of business due to some unforeseen circumstances or exceptional business, a requisition should be prepared and sent direct to the cellar. If the cellar is closed, the duty food and beverage controller will normally sign out the cellar keys, stating the reason, and issue the stock required from the cellar. The keys to the cellar must be returned immediately.

# Receipt of stock into bars

When the stock for the bar is received the barman will check the stock against Parts 2 and 3 of the requisition and if correct sign both copies. Part 3 is retained in the bar for reference and forwarded with other requisitions at the end of the week. Part 2 is sent immediately to the food and beverage controllers, where it is used to compile a consumption analysis sheet.

# Transfers between bars

Stock should be transferred between bars in exceptional circumstances only, and a stock transfer note (Fig. 9.5) in triplicate should be completed and all three copies signed by the barman requesting the transfer. The barman who is making the transfer signs the two top copies, retains one and he sends it with the normal requisitions for his bar to the food and beverage controller; the second copy with the items goes back to the barman requesting the transfer, and this copy goes with the requisitions for that bar to the food and beverage controller. The third copy of the stock transfer note goes to the bar manager for information.

Fig. 9.5    Stock transfer note

| Stock Transfer Note | | NUMBER | | |
| --- | --- | --- | --- | --- |
| | | DATE | | |
| TO | | FROM | | |
| CODE NO. | QUANTITY | ITEM | UNIT VALUE | VALUE |
| | | | | |
| | | | | |
| | | | | |
| | | | | |
| | | | | |
| BARMAN REQUESTING TRANSFER | | BARMAN RECEIVING ITEM | | |
| SIGNATURE | | SIGNATURE | | |

## Mobile bars

Mobile bars for room service or banquets are prepared by the issue of stock from fixed or dispense bars, and strict control must be exercised over issues. A special requisition form in triplicate (Fig. 9.6) should be completed by the person requiring the stock. The barman issuing the stock retains the top and second copies until the balance of the stock is returned. The three copies of the requisition are married together, the stock returned is deducted from the stock issued, the balance being the stock sold. The top copy is passed to the food and beverage controller, the second copy is passed to the bar manager for information, and the third copy is used by room service or banqueting to raise a charging document to the customer or guest as required.

| CODE NO. | ITEM | QUANTITY | UNIT VALUE | ISSUED | | RETURNED | | CONSUMED | | TOTAL VALUE |
|---|---|---|---|---|---|---|---|---|---|---|
| | | | | FULL | NIPS | FULL | NIPS | FULL | NIPS | |
| | | | | | | | | | | |
| | | | | | | | | | | |
| | | | | | | | | | | |
| | | | | | | | | | | |
| | | | | | | | | | | |
| | | | | | | | | | | |
| | TOTALS | | | | | | | | | |

Mobile Bar Requisition — NUMBER — DATE

ISSUING BAR — RECEIVED BY — RETURNED BY — CHARGED TO

SIGNATURE — SIGNATURE — SIGNATURE — SIGNATURE

Fig. 9.6   Mobile bar requisition

# Bottle sales (Fig. 9.7)

Full bottles of spirits or wines are sometimes sold by some bars, room service or banqueting. A daily record should be kept of the sale of all full bottles of liquor or wine so that the food and beverage controller and bar managers can analyse the sales and make allowance for the sales potential on these items.

Fig. 9.7   Full bottle sales record

Bottle Sales — NUMBER — DATE

| CODE NO. | QUANTITY | ITEM | UNIT VALUE | SALES TOTAL | UNIT SALES POTENTIAL | ALLOWANCE £   p |
|---|---|---|---|---|---|---|
| C.K1. | 1 bott. | Whisky | 30p per nip | 4.00 per bott. | £9.60 | £5.60 |
| | | | | | | |
| | | | | | | |
| | | | | | | |
| | | | | | | |
| TOTAL | | | | | | |

BARMAN — FOOD AND BEVERAGE CONTROLLER

133

# The ullage/spillage & breakage book (Fig. 9.8)

The term *ullage* strictly means the unusable portion of a cask of beer, containing sediment, etc., or that used for testing clarity and taste when the cask is broached. Now it denotes all natural losses of liquor.

A record must be kept for all losses through ullage/spillage or breakage, for this must be taken into consideration when ascertaining bar results. An ullage and breakage book is kept, usually in duplicate; bar managers or food and beverage controllers will see the physical evidence where available and countersign the book, and the top copy is passed to the food and beverage controller daily.

Fig. 9.8   Ullage, spillage and breakages record

| CODE NO. | QUANTITY | ITEM | UNIT VALUE | TOTAL COST | REMARKS |
|---|---|---|---|---|---|
| | | **Usage, Spillage and Breakages**   NUMBER / DATE | | | |
| | | | | | |
| BAR / BARTENDER | | | VERIFIED BY | | |

# Beverage purchases analysis book (Fig. 9.9)

To assist the food and beverage controller to evaluate and analyse the expenditure on purchases, a beverage purchase analysis book should be maintained. Delivery notes from suppliers, copy orders and invoices are married together and checked, in particular the prices; this is done by referring to the price lists, which should always be kept up to date. Details from the invoices are entered, analysed and totalled, and this will produce the total expenditure on each type of beverage. These figures are studied by the controllers and any deviations from the normal will call for investigation and if necessary corrective action. As containers are normally charged on invoices, and when returned Credit Notes are received for the containers returned, it is necessary to have columns showing this in the purchases analysis book.

## Beverages Purchases Analysis Book

| DATE | COPY ORDER NUMBER | SUPPLIER | INVOICE NUMBER | BEER | MINERALS | SPIRITS | WINES | TOTAL | CONTAINERS DR | CR | NET TOTAL |
|------|-------------------|----------|----------------|------|----------|---------|-------|-------|---------------|-----|-----------|
| | | | | ① | ② | ③ | ④ | ⑤ | ⑥ | ⑦ | ⑧ |
| | | | | | | | | ⑤ = ① + ② + ③ + ④ | | | ⑧ = ⑤ + ⑥ − ⑦ |

Fig. 9.9    Beverage purchases analysis book

# Beverage control book (Fig. 9.10)

A beverage control book will exercise an overall check on the receivals and issues in terms of actual value and also provide a basis for checking the cellar inventory. The value of opening stock plus total purchases (including value of containers received less value of containers returned), less total of issues to individual bars, will equal the closing stock.

Fig. 9.10    Beverage control book

## Beverage Control Book

| DATE | OPENING STOCK £ p | PURCHASES £ p | CONTAINER RECEIVED £ p | RETURNED £ p | NET PURCHASES £ p | ISSUES TO BAR LOUNGE BAR £ p | COCKTAIL BAR £ p | BLUE ROOM BAR £ p | OTHERS £ p | TOTAL ISSUES £ p |
|------|------|------|------|------|------|------|------|------|------|------|
| | | | | | | | | | | |

# Analysed stock records (Fig. 9.11)

Analysed stock record cards will provide details of the issues made to each individual outlet and can be used as a check on the bar consumption for the individual bars. They can also be used as a check on the stock records maintained in the cellars. Details of goods received are obtained from delivery notes from suppliers; issues are entered from the bar requisitions, the daily balance is increased when items are received and decreased when items are issued to the various outlets.

Fig. 9.11 Analysed stock record card

### Stock Record Card

BIN NUMBER 3  
ITEM Gordons Gin  MINIMUM STOCK 24  
MAXIMUM STOCK 48  RE-ORDER POINT 36  
SUPPLIER T.W. Smithers + Co.

| DATE | RECEIVALS | LOUNGE BAR | BANQUETING | DISPENSE BAR | COCKTAIL BAR | BLUE ROOM BAR | TARTAN BAR | ROOM SERVICE | NIGHT SERVICE | KITCHEN | TOTAL ISSUES | BALANCE |
|------|-----------|------------|------------|--------------|--------------|---------------|------------|--------------|---------------|---------|--------------|---------|
| 197. Jan. 1 | | | | | | | | | | | | 36 |
| 2 | 12 | | | | | | | | | | | 48 |
| 2 | | 1 | | | 2 | | | 1 | 1 | 1 | | 42 |

Fig. 9.12 Bar consumption summary sheet

### Bar Consumption Summary Sheet

| ITEM | MEASURES PER BOTT | UNIT COST | OPENING STOCK | ISSUES | CLOSING STOCK | TOTAL CONSUMED | TOTAL COST | UNIT SELLING PRICE | TOTAL SALES | GROSS PROFIT % |
|------|-------------------|-----------|---------------|--------|---------------|----------------|------------|--------------------|-------------|----------------|
| Gin | 32 | 3.20 | 4 | 2 | 2 | 4 | 12.80 | 25p per nip | 32.00 | 60% |
| Sherry | 12 | 1.25 | 2 | 6 | 3 | 5 | 6.25 | 22p per glass | 13.20 | 52.6% |
| Beer | 1 x 10 gal. | 8.50 | 1 x 10 gal. | 1 x 10 gal. | 5/10 gal. | 19 5/10 gal. | 16.57½ | 24p per pint | 37.44 | 55.7% |
| | | | | | | | 35.62½ | | 82.64 | |

SUMMARY  
A TOTAL COST £35.62½  
B TOTAL SALES £82.64  
C GROSS PROFIT £47.01½  
D GROSS PROFIT % 56.8%

## Bar consumption summary sheets (Fig. 9.12)

The results of each bar are summarised on bar consumption sheets. Opening stock at the commencement of business, plus issues to the bar on requisition, less stock at the end of business, will equal stock consumed.

# Control of bar stock at selling price

In the fixed bars, in order to reconcile the value of stock consumed with the actual takings in the till, issues to the fixed bar are valued at cost price and at potential selling price.

## Method

1. The master wine list will provide the selling price of each item.
2. Potential selling prices of the bottles will be calculated by multiplying the price per glass or measure by the number of glasses in the bottle.

| Example: | Measures per bot. | Selling price per measure | Potential selling price per bottle |
|---|---|---|---|
| 1 bot. whisky | 32 | 30p per nip | £9·60 |

3. By using measuring sticks, opened bottles can be valued at the proportion remaining compared with the number of glasses which can be produced from a full bottle.
4. Wines sold by the bottle are valued at the price stated on the master wine list.
5. For cross-checking purposes, an additional column showing the potential selling price of stock can be added to the stock record cards, stock sheets and purchases day book.

## Mixed drinks

When stock is valued at the selling price, if the reconciliation of the stock consumed with the takings in the till results in a discrepancy, immediate investigation is called for. A surplus can normally be expected for the following reasons.

1. Bottles of beer and bottles of lemonade are individually valued at the selling price, but when mixed together as shandies the ingredients mixed may amount to a different selling price.
2. Spirits mixed with tonic, orange, bitters, soda, etc., may result in a surplus, as the selling price of the mixed drink may not be in proportion to the ingredients.
3. The selling prices of bottles of fortified wine (75 cl) may be calculated on a yield of 12 glasses per bottle but in practice they may yield 14–16 glasses.

# Allowances

When fixed bars are being strictly controlled on a selling price basis, it must be remembered that adjustment must be made on the bar consumption summary sheet for any of the following:

1. Any transfers between bars
2. Any ullages or breakages
3. Bottle sales
4. Issues to staff
5. Hospitality drinks
6. Withdrawals by proprietors.

# Calculation of gross profit on bars

By a simple calculation it is possible to reconcile stock consumed with the sales figures, to calculate the gross profit percentage on each outlet, and highlight any surplus, discrepancies or variances from normal.

*Example 1:*

*Blue Room Bar*
for week ending 7 July 19..

| | £ | £ |
|---|---|---|
| Sales | | 550 |
| Opening stock at cost price | 29 | |
| *Plus* Issues at cost price | 232 | |
| | 261 | |
| *Less* Closing stock at cost price | 30 | |
| Stock consumed | | 231 |
| Gross profit | | £319 |
| Gross profit % | | 58% |

# *Calculations of surplus/discrepancies percentages*

*Example 2:*

*Blue Room Bar*
for week ending 7 July 19..

| | £ | £ |
|---|---|---|
| Sales | | 550 |
| Opening stock at selling price | 45 | |
| *Add* Issues at selling price | 518 | |
| | 563 | |
| *Less* Closing stock at selling price | 21 | |
| | | 542 |
| Surplus | | £8 |

*Example 3:*                     *Blue Room Bar*
                      for week ending 31 July 19. .

|                                              | £   | £   |
|----------------------------------------------|-----|-----|
| Sales                                        |     | 721 |
| Opening stock at selling price               | 24  |     |
| *Add* Issues at selling price                | 714 |     |
| *Add* Transfers into bar at selling price    | 20  |     |
|                                              | 758 |     |

|                                                | £   |     |     |
|------------------------------------------------|-----|-----|-----|
| *Less* Closing stock at selling price          | 38  |     |     |
| *Less* Transfers out of bar at selling price   | 12  |     |     |
| *Less* Allowances                              | 8   | 58  |     |
| Stock consumed                                 |     |     | 700 |
| Surplus                                        |     |     | £21 |

Surplus %                     $\dfrac{21}{700} \times 100 = 3\%$

# Stocktaking and stock checks

Physical stock checks of the cellar and all bars should be carried out at
regular intervals by the food and beverage controllers or by specially
appointed stocktakers. Lists of all stocks held by the cellar and all bars
should be prepared, valued and verified and any significant differences
must be notified to the bar managers.

Spot checks of a surprise nature should be carried out on each bar and
in the cellar by the controller; to be effective the bar and cellar staff should
be given no prior notice of such checks.

| Bar: |
| Date: |

| Bin no. | Item | Par stock | No. of measures | Cost price £ | Selling price £ | Gross profit £ % | |
|---|---|---|---|---|---|---|---|
| | Whisky | | 32 | | | | |
| | Gin | | 32 | | | | |
| | Vermouth | | 19 | | | | |
| | Sherry | | 16 | | | | |
| | Dubonnet | | 21 | | | | |
| | Brandy | | 32 | | | | |
| | Vodka | | 32 | | | | |
| | Cherry brandy | | 32 | | | | |
| | Beer | | | | | | |
| | Wines | | | | | | |
| | Squashes | | | | | | |
| | Cigarettes Cigars | | | | | | |
| | | | | | Signature of bar manager | | |

## Bar inventory list (Fig. 9.13)

Each bar will have a 'bar inventory list' prepared showing details of the stock 'par' of each item carried by the bar. These are used when the stock is physically counted; the closing stock of each item is entered on the bar inventory list, and this will automatically become the opening stock for the next trading period.

| Bar Inventory List | | | | | | | |
|---|---|---|---|---|---|---|---|
| BAR Blue Room<br>DATE | | | | | | | |
| BIN<br>NO. | ITEM | PAR<br>STOCK | UNIT<br>VALUE | CLOSING<br>STOCK | COST<br>VALUE | SELLING PRICE<br>VALUE | |
| | | | | | | | |
| CHECKED BY | | | | | FOOD AND BEVERAGE CONTROLLER | | |

Fig. 9.13   Bar inventory list

# Frauds in bars

The perpetration of fraud is not always caused by someone acting out of necessity, but with some misguided persons it amounts to almost a game against the establishment. Whatever the reason for the fraud, the establishment not only stands to lose the value of the items misappropriated but also the profit that would have been made by the sale of such items. There is no complete anti-fraud system, but by careful selection of staff, constant vigilance, strict control systems, and an awareness of the types of fraud that can be perpetrated, a great measure of control can be exercised. It is one of the main functions of a controller to ensure that all control procedures in operation are strictly adhered to by all members of staff.

## 1. *Short measure*

If stock control in a bar is based on a selling-price basis, the barman will only have to account in the till for the value of the stock sold. By giving short measures of drink to customers, a greater yield per bottle can be obtained and the barman can pocket the difference. The controller should visit the bar in busy periods, be watchful, ensure that all sales are rung up on the till and listen for complaints from customers about short measure, as not only must the fraud be curbed but this kind of practice will promote bad will for the establishment and could result in prosecution or a loss of custom.

## 2. Short-changing

Price lists should be displayed prominently in the bars, and any complaint of short-changing or overcharging by a barman should be investigated.

## 3. Ringing up the wrong amounts

Few customers observe the price rung up on the till or listen for the ring which indicates that the till drawer is being opened and closed when each item is being registered; therefore it is not difficult for a barman to ring up a lesser amount or omit to ring up any amount, and thus make a handy profit for himself. Controllers must watch for this practice and visit the bars regularly to observe.

## 4. Dilution

By watering drinks a barman can produce more-than-average measures from the bottles and take the additional revenue himself. By using a hydrometer the controller can do spot checks on the gravity or 'proof' of liquor, which will detect any watering down of spirits.

## 5. Adulteration

An experienced barman can adulterate drinks such as sherry or liqueurs with cheaper types of drink, making a profit on the sale which he will pocket. A keen eye and palate on the part of the controller when sampling will be an important defence against frauds of this nature.

## 6. Mixing drinks

Mixing expensive spirits with cheaper, especially when mixing cocktails could produce additional revenue which could be skimmed off by the barman.

## 7. Carrying in bottles

By carrying in their own stocks of liquor and selling it at the bar, the barmen can make a personal profit. The controller, when analysing the results of the bar, should watch for a falling off in sales and note unusually high sales of tonics or sodas, etc., without a relative consumption of spirits. A watchful eye must be kept for strange bottles not normally stocked by the establishment.

## 8. Stock substitution

In the cellar and the bars, the stock checkers must always look behind the façade. All bottles should be examined carefully, seals should be checked, bottles wrapped in tissue paper should be unwrapped, and the back of shelves of stock checked as water can be substituted for beer and tea for whisky. Hypodermic needles can go through corks and draw off measures of liquor, and crown tops can be removed and replaced by experts to look undisturbed. Cellarmen or barmen perpetrating this type of fraud show reluctance to allow anyone else to handle their stock and to take holidays or take time off work.

## 9. Chargeable containers

Strict control should be exercised over returnable containers, as dishonest cellarmen and deliverymen can have a method of disposing of containers to their own personal benefit. Controllers must check that credits are received for all returnable containers.

## 10. Altering requisitions

All copies of requisitions should be married together and the figures on each should be checked, as it is a simple matter for a 3 to be altered to an 8 or a 0 to a 9 when withdrawing stock from the cellar or bar.

## 11. Cigarettes and tobacco

As cigarettes and tobacco yield a low gross profit margin on their sales, it is desirable that they should be isolated from the bar trading result, otherwise the bar's overall gross profit percentage would be reduced if there was a high turnover in tobacco sales.

To get a more accurate trading result, a fixed par stock costed at retail selling price is set up for each bar. A separate cash float is operated. A rapid check at the end of each session should result in stock at start, plus receivals into stocks, less stock at end being equal to the cigarette and tobacco takings plus the cash float.

As cigarettes and tobacco are of high value and small bulk, they are easily pilfered; therefore strict control over stocks should be exercised at all times and it is generally felt that the use of vending machines is the simplest method of preventing fraud.

# Progress test questions

1. What is the purpose of the master wine list and what information will it provide?
2. Outline briefly basic purchasing procedures when ordering stock for the cellar.
3. Outline the responsibilities and duties of the receiving clerk.
4. Outline the responsibilities and duties of the head cellarman and his staff on receiving goods into the cellar.
5. Detail cellar procedures with regard to the issue of stock.
6. Discuss the methods of controlling stock in fixed bars.
7. Detail procedures for the issue of stock to mobile bars.
8. What information will an analysed purchases book provide for the food and beverage controller?
9. Explain the purpose of the beverage control book.
10. Illustrate with a diagram an analysed stock record card.
11. From the following information calculate the percentage surplus or discrepancy for the Tartan Bar for the week ending 30 June 19 . .: Issues at selling price £490, Opening stock at selling price £21, Closing stock at selling price £9, Takings in the bar for the week £498.
12. Calculate the gross profit percentage for the Tartan Bar for the week ending 30 June 19 . . from the following information: Takings for the week £498, Opening stock at cost price £10, Closing stock at cost price £4, Issues at cost price £233.
13. Calculate the percentage surplus or discrepancy for the Green Room Bar for the week ending 20 September 19 . . from the following information: Sales £947, Opening stock at selling price £120, Closing stock at selling price £87, Issues at selling price £861, Transfers into the bar at selling price £35, Allowances £12, Transfers out of the bar at selling price £42.
14. From the following information prepare a 'Bar Consumption Summary Sheet' (as per Fig. 9.12):

| Measures per bott. | Item | Opening stock | Closing stock | Issues | Unit cost | Unit selling price |
|---|---|---|---|---|---|---|
| 32 | Gin | 3 bott. | 2 bott. | 3 bott. | £3·30 per bot. | 30p per nip |
| 32 | Whisky | 2 bott. | 1 bott. | 4 bott. | £3·50 per bot. | 35p per nip |
| 13 | Sherry | 4 bott. | 6 bott. | 2 bott. | £1·40 per bot. | 28p per glass |

15. A food and beverage controller must always be aware of the possibility of fraud. Discuss this statement, mentioning the types of fraud that can be perpetrated and methods of prevention.

# CHAPTER 10

# Cash Control

The sale of food, beverages or accommodation can be either for cash or credit. Sales can be made by the waiters in the restaurant, the wine waiters, over the counter at the bar, by the lounge waiters or room service waiters. Control must be exercised to ensure that whenever a sale is made it results in either cash in the till or as a charge on a customer's account.

## Sales recorded through tills

1. Every sale that is made by payment of cash through a till must be recorded by operating appropriate keys on the machine. If there are facilities on the keyboard to analyse the sale, care must be taken that the correct keys are used.
2. Most till drawers ring a bell when opened and the ear should be alerted to that ring, for no till drawer should be left open between sales as that would be an open invitation to a thief.
3. At the end of the shift or service the cash is removed from the till and the float separated from the takings.
4. The barman or cashier has the responsibility of completing the *cashing-up return* (Fig. 10.1). This return will show:
   (a) Opening till reading
   (b) Closing till reading
   (c) Total cash sales
   (d) Total credit sales
   (e) Details of credit sales and transfers to other outlets for which no cash is received
   (f) List of any cheques received
   (g) Cash summary on reverse (Fig. 10.2)
   (h) Signature of person paying the cash
   (i) Signature of person receiving the cash.
5. After completing the cashing-up slip, it is taken with the cash and all top copies of the credit bills to the billing office.
6. The cashier in the billing office will check the cash and the analysis on the cashing-up slip and if correct will sign for cash received. The top copies of the credit bills are used to bill the customer.
7. The cashing-up sheet and credit bills are then forwarded to the food and beverage controllers who will match them to the second copies received from the various outlets.
8. Food and beverage controllers must read every till at the

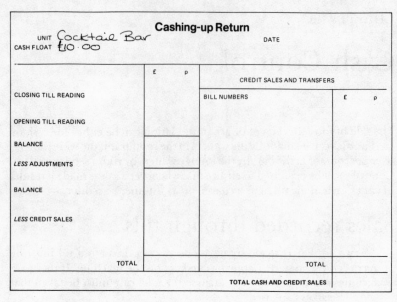

## Cashing-up Return

UNIT *Cocktail Bar*
CASH FLOAT *£10·00*
DATE

|  | £ | p | CREDIT SALES AND TRANSFERS | | |
|---|---|---|---|---|---|
|  |  |  | BILL NUMBERS | £ | p |
| CLOSING TILL READING |  |  |  |  |  |
| OPENING TILL READING |  |  |  |  |  |
| BALANCE |  |  |  |  |  |
| *LESS* ADJUSTMENTS |  |  |  |  |  |
| BALANCE |  |  |  |  |  |
| *LESS* CREDIT SALES |  |  |  |  |  |
| TOTAL |  |  | TOTAL |  |  |
|  |  |  | TOTAL CASH AND CREDIT SALES |  |  |

Fig. 10.1   Cashing-up return (front)

Fig. 10.2   Cashing-up return (reverse)

## Cash Summary

|  | £ | p |  | £ | p |
|---|---|---|---|---|---|
| CREDIT CARD *AND CHEQUES* |  |  | TOTAL CHEQUES |  |  |
|  |  |  | £10 |  |  |
|  |  |  | £5 |  |  |
|  |  |  | £1 |  |  |
|  |  |  | 50p |  |  |
|  |  |  | 10p |  |  |
|  |  |  | 5p |  |  |
|  |  |  | 2p |  |  |
|  |  |  | 1p |  |  |
|  |  |  | TOTAL |  |  |
|  |  |  | *LESS* FLOAT |  |  |
|  |  |  | CASH TAKINGS |  |  |
| PAID BY SIGNATURE |  |  | OVER |  |  |
| RECEIVED BY SIGNATURE |  |  | SHORT |  |  |

commencement of business and at the end of every shift. Till readings must be entered on the cashing-up slips and agreed with the analysis of the day's business.

# Credit sales—room service

1. Room service sales are controlled by using the triple checking system. The order for food or beverage is taken and the top copy of the check pad is used to obtain the required items from the kitchen, dispense bar or stillroom.
2. The guest signs the second copy of the waiter's check on receipt of the items; it is then passed to the billing office, where it is used to charge the customer's account. The billing office enters all checks on an analysis sheet, which is passed with the checks to the food and beverage controllers.
3. The third copy is used to write up the room service control sheet (Fig. 10.3), which is passed with the checks to the food and beverage controllers.
4. The food and beverage controllers match the top copy from the bar, stillroom or kitchen with the second copy from the billing office and the third copy from the room service control check pad. The analysis sheets from each point are also cross-checked.

Fig. 10.3   Room service control sheet

| | | | | | FOOD | | | | | DRINKS | | | | BILLING OFFICE CREDIT |
|---|---|---|---|---|---|---|---|---|---|---|---|---|---|---|
| **Room Service Control Sheet** DATE | | | | | | | | | | | | | | |
| BILL NO. | WAITER'S NO. | NAME | ROOM NO. | NO. OF COVERS | B FAST | LUNCH | DINNER | TEA | SUNDRY | BAR ACCOUNT | DISPENSE BAR | TOBACCO | CASH | |
| | | | | | | | | | | | | | | |
| | | | | | | | | | | | | | | |
| | | | | | | | | | | | | | | |
| | | | | | | | | | | | | | | |
| | | | | | | | | | | | | | | |

# Cash and credit sales in the restaurant

1. For control in the restaurant the triplicate check pad is used by the waiters. Each pad has an identifying serial number. The *top* copy is handed into the kitchen or bar for the order. The *second* copy is passed to the cashier who uses it to compile the customer's bill. The *third* copy is retained by the waiter and at the end of service passed to the food and beverage controller.
2. The cashier's bills (Fig. 10.4) are numbered consecutively and made out in duplicate. If an error is made on a bill, the word 'cancelled' should be written across its face and it should be filed in its correct number order.

3. The top copy is receipted by the cashier if the customer pays cash. If the bill is to be charged to an account, the customer will sign the bill and it will be returned to the cashier.
4. At the end of service the cashier will prepare from the cash and credit bills an analysed summary sheet (Fig. 10.5), which will be passed together with the cash and copies of bills to cashier in the billing office.
5. The cashier will check the cash, the bills and the summary sheet.
6. Credit bills will be used for entry on to the tabular ledger and guests' accounts.
7. In the control office the top copies of the waiters' checks from the kitchen and bars, together with the second copies from the cashiers, are cross-checked against duplicates of the paid bills, credit bills and summary sheets to ensure that pricing is correct and that everything has been charged.

Fig. 10.4   Cashier's bill

| | | | | |
|---|---|---|---|---|
| **Bill** | | | | |
| | JAMESVILLE HOTEL EASTGATE | | | |
| TABLE NUMBER *1* NO. OF COVERS *4* | | BILL NUMBER *1021* DATE *15.4.19--* | | |
| | | | £ | p |
| | 4 Lunches @ £2.50 | | 10. | 00 |
| | Drinks @ £3.20 | | 3. | 20 |
| | | | 13. | 20 |
| | Service Charge 10% | | 1. | 32 |
| | | | 14. | 52 |
| | V.A.T. 8% | | 1. | 08 |
| VAT REGISTRATION NUMBER 121 3126 30 | | TOTAL | £15. | 60 |

# Value Added Tax

Various types of tax are levied in most countries. In the United Kingdom Value Added Tax has to be paid to H.M. Customs and Excise and is levied on most goods and services. There are certain exemptions classified as exempted or Zero Rated, and two rates of tax, standard rate and special rate.

V.A.T. came into operation in the U.K. on 1 April 1973, the standard rate being 10%; from 28 July 1974 the standard rate was reduced to 8%, and as the Treasury retains the power to increase or decrease the percentages, the rates could vary at any time.

Some hoteliers and caterers quote their tariff prices for meals and accommodation as V.A.T. inclusive, which means that the Value Added Tax is included in the charge. Others quote their prices as V.A.T. exclusive, and Value Added Tax is added after the bill has been totalled.

The law requires that V.A.T. is forwarded at regular intervals to H.M. Customs and Excise, therefore accurate records must be kept of the tax collected, and cashiers should understand the basic principles of calculating V.A.T., whatever the percentage.

*Calculation:*

*V.A.T. Inclusive*

*The bill* + *V.A.T.*

$(100\%) + (8\%) = 108\%$

Therefore The bill $= \dfrac{100}{108} = \dfrac{25}{27}$

Therefore V.A.T. $= \dfrac{8}{108} = \dfrac{2}{27}$

---

Fig. 10.5   Cashier's analysis sheet

Restaurant
Last bill no.: 1020                                                     Date: 16.4.19..

| Bill no. | Table no. | No. of covers | Food £ | Drink £ | Service 10% £ | Sub-total £ | V.A.T. £ | Total cash sales £ |
|---|---|---|---|---|---|---|---|---|
| 1021 | 1 | 4 | 10·00 | 3·20 | 1·32 | 14·52 | 1·16 | 15·68 |
| 1022 | 6 | 3 | 7·50 | 1·25 | 0·88 | 9·63 | 0·77 | 10·40 |
| 1024 | 12 | 6 | 15·00 | 4·20 | 1·92 | 21·12 | 1·69 | 22·81 |
| 1025 | 2 | 2 | 5·00 | 0·90 | 0·59 | 6·49 | 0·52 | 7·01 |
| 1026 | 4 | 2 | 5·00 | 1·10 | 0·61 | 6·71 | 0·54 | 7·25 |
| 1028 | 9 | 4 | 10·00 | 3·15 | 1·32 | 14·47 | 1·16 | 15·63 |
| 1029 | 8 | 4 | 10·00 | 2·20 | 1·22 | 13·42 | 1·07 | 14·49 |
| 1031 | 5 | 8 | 20·00 | 7·20 | 2·72 | 29·92 | 2·39 | 32·31 |
| 1032 | 13 | 2 | 5·00 | 0·80 | 0·58 | 6·38 | 0·51 | 6·89 |
| 1033 | 10 | 3 | 7·50 | 1·80 | 0·93 | 10·23 | 0·82 | 11·05 |
| 1034 | 14 | 4 | 10·00 | 2·60 | 1·26 | 13·86 | 1·11 | 14·97 |
| Totals | | 42 | 105·00 | 28·40 | 13·35 | 146·75 | 11·74 | 158·49 |

Check:

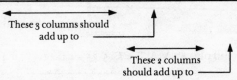

These 3 columns should add up to

These 2 columns should add up to

## Credit bills

| Bill no. | Table no. | No. of covers | Food £ | Drink £ | Total £ | Name | Room no. |
|---|---|---|---|---|---|---|---|
| 1023 | 11 | 4 | 10·00 | 3·20 | 13·20 | Mr R. James | 103 |
| 1027 | 7 | 2 | 5·00 | 0·90 | 5·90 | Mr L. Sales | 105 |
| 1030 | 2 | 2 | 5·00 | 1·40 | 6·40 | Mrs M. Horton | 207 |
| Totals | | 8 | 20·00 | 5·50 | 25·50 | | |

Check:

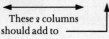

These 2 columns should add to

| | | £ | | | £ |
|---|---|---|---|---|---|
| Cash analysis | £5 | 65·00 | Cheques bill no. 1031 | | £32·31 |
| | £1 | 55·00 | White—Bankers' Card | | |
| | 50p | 3·00 | no. 236741 | | |
| | 10p | 2·60 | | | |
| | 5p | 0·25 | | | |
| | 2p | 0·28 | | | |
| | 1p | 0·05 | | | |
| | | 126·18 | Paid in by _____ | | |
| N.B. Total cash should agree with total cash sales | Cheque | 32·31 | Checked by _____ | | |
| | | 158·49 | | | |

---

*Example 1:*

### V.A.T. inclusive bill

Bill = £16·47 V.A.T. inclusive

To calculate V.A.T.:  $\dfrac{2}{27} = 9)\ \overline{16·47}$    $3)\ \overline{1·83}$

$0·61 \times 2 = £1·22$

| | £ |
|---|---|
| Bill | 16·47 |
| *Less* V.A.T. | 1·22 |
| V.A.T. exclusive | £15·25 |

To check: Bill    £15·25 + 8%

$\times\ \ 0·08$

£1·22  (move decimal point 2 places to left)

Bill plus 8% V.A.T. = £15·25 + £1·22 = £16·47

# Cheques

Cashiers asked to accept cheques in settlement of bills or accounts should note the following points:

1. Cheques exceeding the limit laid down by management must be approved before being accepted.
2. The date should be checked; the cheque must not be 'stale' which means more than six months old, or post-dated, which means a future date.
3. The hotel must be named as the payee.
4. The words and figures must agree; any alterations must be signed by the drawer.
5. The cheque must be signed.
6. Identification should be obtained, i.e. bankers card, the number of which should be written on the back of the cheque.

# Credit cards

In the early 1950s credit cards and widespread credit in general began gaining great impetus, and many hotels, restaurants and other businesses are prepared to give credit facilities to holders of credit cards. These cards are issued by large organisations such as the American Express Company, Diner's Club, Barclays Bank and others to business and professional men and other persons who travel frequently. Membership requires a rigid credit investigation, as the organisation guarantees the payment of bills run up by the credit card holders.

A plastic embossed card shows details of the holder's name and account number, which are impressed on a slip which the holder signs for goods and services received. Where it is the policy of an establishment to accept credit cards, staff must ensure that the signature of the person signing checks against the signature on the credit cards and the card itself must not be out of date.

Usually at the end of each month credit card numbers and the amounts spent by the holders are listed and sent with the relevant slips to the respective credit card companies who reimburse the retailers with the amounts due less a fixed commission which they retain to cover their risk, administrative expenses and profit. They in turn collect the debts from the credit card holders.

# Cash floats

These are certain sums of money handed out to the sales outlets such as the restaurants and bars so that they may have change available at the start of business. Cash floats must be checked and signed for when distributed in the mornings. At the close of each shift or service, when the takings are

Fig. 10.6  Analysed petty cash book

| Cash received | Date | Details | Voucher No. | Total | Postage and telegrams | Printing and stationery | Travelling expenses | Flowers and garden | Entertainment | Repairs and maintenance | Gratuities | Cleaning materials | Uniform cleaning | Sundry items | Provisions | Casual wages | Visitors paid out |
|---|---|---|---|---|---|---|---|---|---|---|---|---|---|---|---|---|---|
| £ | 19.. |  |  | £ | £ | £ | £ | £ | £ | £ | £ | £ | £ | £ | £ | £ | £ |
| 30·00 | Jan. 1 | Imprest | — | — |  |  |  |  |  |  |  |  |  |  |  |  |  |
|  | ,, 1 | Postage | 1 | 4·00 | 4·00 |  |  |  |  |  |  |  |  |  |  |  |  |
|  | ,, 2 | Travelling expenses | 2 | 1·50 |  |  | 1·50 |  |  |  |  |  |  |  |  |  |  |
|  | ,, 2 | Flowers | 3 | 2·00 |  |  |  | 2·00 |  |  |  |  |  |  |  |  |  |
|  | ,, 3 | Mr. Brown—Rm. 12 |  |  |  |  |  |  |  |  |  |  |  |  |  |  |  |
|  |  | Taxi | 4 | 0·60 |  |  |  |  |  |  |  |  |  |  |  |  | 0·60 |
|  | ,, 4 | Magazines | 5 | 1·20 |  |  |  |  |  |  |  |  |  | 1·20 |  |  |  |
|  | ,, 4 | Provisions | 6 | 2·30 |  |  |  |  |  |  |  |  |  |  | 2·30 |  |  |
|  | ,, 5 | Band | 7 | 12·00 |  |  |  |  | 12·00 |  |  |  |  |  |  |  |  |
|  | ,, 5 | Casual wages | 8 | 5·00 |  |  |  |  |  |  |  |  |  |  |  | 5·00 |  |
|  | ,, 6 | Mr. Jones—Rm. 8 | 9 | 0·35 |  |  |  |  |  |  |  |  |  |  |  |  | 0·35 |
|  | ,, 6 | Tip—delivery man | 10 | 0·20 |  |  |  |  |  |  | 0·20 |  |  |  |  |  |  |
|  |  |  |  | 29·15 | 4·00 | — | 1·50 | 2·00 | 12·00 | — | 0·20 | — | — | 1·20 | 2·30 | 5·00 | 0·95 |
|  | Jan. 7 | Balance | c/d | 0·85 |  |  |  |  |  |  |  |  |  |  |  |  |  |
| 30·00 |  |  |  | 30·00 |  |  |  |  |  |  |  |  |  |  |  |  |  |
| 0·85 | Jan. 7 | Balance | b/d | — |  |  |  |  |  |  |  |  |  |  |  |  |  |
| 29·15 | ,, 7 | Reimbursing cash |  | — |  |  |  |  |  |  |  |  |  |  |  |  |  |

ANALYSIS

collected and checked, the float is extracted. Cash floats should be re-checked and distributed again at the commencement of the next service or shift.

# Petty cash control

Most businesses incur small petty cash payments for various items which, during the course of time, can amount to a considerable expenditure. The most effective way of controlling petty cash for small or medium-sized establishments is by the imprest system, whereby the petty cashier is entrusted with a fixed sum of money called the 'imprest', out of which all small payments are made. An analysed Petty Cash Book is kept (Fig. 10.6), which will provide details of the total amounts spent on each type of expense. These totals are then posted from the petty cash book to the correct account in the ledger. Periodically the petty cash book, receipts and vouchers are presented to the chief cashier for audit, and if correct the petty cashier will be re-imbursed with the amount spent, thus bringing the petty cash back to the original imprest.

## Advantages of the system

1. Any theft will be limited to the amount of the 'imprest'.
2. Small items are kept out of the cash book.
3. The petty cashier has the responsibility of accounting for a fixed sum of money.
4. Control is exercised over small items of expenditure, which can mount up during the accounting period.
5. There is a regular audit on petty cash expenditure.
6. The recipient of the cash must sign a petty cash voucher acknowledging receipt of the money.

## Petty cash float

In some large hotels using machine accounting, where it would be impractical to keep a petty cash book as such because of the volume of payments, an imprest or cash float is still used for petty cash payments. At the end of each week the signed petty cash vouchers are sorted under their respective headings of expenditure, numbered consecutively and machine totalled. Each batch of vouchers has the machine total stapled to the front. From these a petty cash summary sheet is prepared showing the total expenditure under its headings and these totals are then posted to their respective accounts.

Fig. 10.7 Petty cash summary sheet

**Petty Cash Summary Sheet**

WEEK ENDING

| ACCOUNT CODE NUMBER | DETAILS | GROSS £  p | VAT £  p | NET £  p | VOUCHER NUMBERS |
|---|---|---|---|---|---|
| | Food Purchases | | | | |
| | Drink Purchases | | | | |
| | Casual Wages | | | | |
| | Uniforms (Cleaning) | | | | |
| | Household (Cleaning) | | | | |
| | Cleaning Materials | | | | |
| | Printing and Stationery | | | | |
| | Postage | | | | |
| | Travelling Expenses | | | | |
| | Newspapers and Magazines | | | | |
| | Flowers and Gardens | | | | |
| | Repairs and Maintenance | | | | |
| | Entertainments | | | | |
| | Staff Engagement Costs | | | | |
| | Staff Training Costs | | | | |
| | Gratuities | | | | |
| | Licences | | | | |
| | Subscriptions | | | | |
| | Donations | | | | |
| | Visitors Paid Outs | | | | |
| | Sundries (Itemised) | | | | |

# Mechanised accounting

A few years ago mechanised hotel systems were practically non-existent; nowadays, however, there are many mechanised systems available to the hotel and catering industry. The extent of mechanisation will depend on the individual hotelier or restaurateur and the needs of his particular operation.

## Advantages of mechanisation

1. *Improved records*—Records prepared by machine are more legible.
2. *Increased speed*—By simultaneous posting operations time and labour can be saved.
3. *Greater accuracy*—Machine posting helps eliminate some of the human error in calculations.
4. *Analysed information* for management is easily produced.

# Electronic cash registers

There are many different types of cash register on the market and many new developments in electronic cash registers. For example, the NCR 210 has a choice of several keyboards and performs the following functions:

### 1. Change of computation
The register automatically prints the total of the sale and the amount tendered and calculates and prints either the change due or the amount still owing. When the register finalises the transactions the drawer opens. Automatic change computation eliminates inaccuracies in making change and speeds customer service.

### 2. Addition and subtraction
With electronic addition and subtraction, the customer's receipt is a printed statement showing the amount of each item purchased and the amount of each credit—whether refunds or discounts.

### 3. Quantity extension
Multiple items that sell for the same price are easily recorded. The number of units and total price are printed on the customer's receipt.

### 4. Single items
Single items can be recorded without going through the programmed sequence of sub-totals. The register prints the customer's receipt, displays the amount and opens the cash drawer.

### 5. Money count
A money key makes it easy to count the money from the drawer when balancing. This allows a quick comparison of the actual money in the drawer with the cash called for by the registered total.

These machines also provide transaction control by the following methods:

### 1. Cash sales
Cash customers receive a machine-printed receipt and can visually check prices on the diaplay as each item is recorded. All cash sales add into a protected total and must be accounted for.

### 2. Charge sales
Charge sales are recorded in the same manner as cash sales and this establishes a protected record of the transaction.

### 3. Money received on account
Moneys received on account are recorded on the register. Accurate

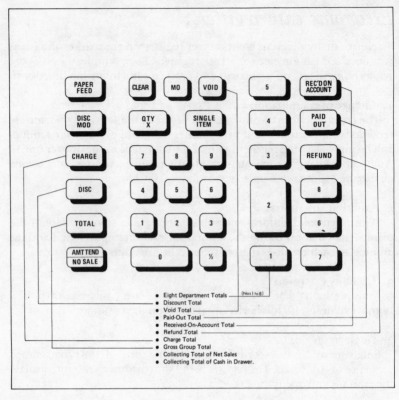

Fig. 10.8　NCR 210 electronic cash register keyboard arrangement (15 totals model)

records of money received on account assure the customer of full credit and establish accountability for the money received.

### 4. Money paid out

Control can be exercised over money paid out by providing printed proof of the amount of each paid out transaction.

### 5. Discount

A discount key can record all discount items. It also accumulates a total of discounts.

### 6. Void operation

Operators can void (cancel) an incorrect entry before finalising a transaction.

### 7. Balance and audit

Each transaction is identified and the printing of voids, refunds, paid outs and negative totals in red pinpoint areas in need of audit. Also it is easier to balance records in the drawer with recordings on the journal.

# Permanent records

Machine accounting can provide permanent printed records for the customer and for the management.

## 1. Receipts

The customer's recipt builds security around every transaction. Itemised receipts assure both customer and management that correct prices have been charged and the transaction has been accurately recorded.

## 2. The journal

A permanent record of every transaction prints in order of occurrence during the business day and the sales journal is under personal control of the management.

## 3. Management information

Dependent on the machine, several printed totals are available—the printed information simplifies balancing and auditing, streamlines office procedures and exercises tighter control while reducing paper work.

# Hotel billing machines

At the time of writing, the NCR 5 Restaurant Billing Machine and the Sweda Billing Machine are the most commonly used, but the manufacturers are constantly making improvements and modifications.

These machines replace the handwritten visitors' ledger. The guest's account is in two parts, the top copy for the guest, the bottom copy as the hotel record. Departmental vouchers issued by the selling departments of the hotel are forwarded to the billing office during the course of the day. Charges from these vouchers are posted to the two copies of the account simultaneously, therefore no discrepancies are possible. Each account is balanced. The top copy is presented to the guest and the bottom copy is used for accounting purposes by the hotel.

# Restaurant accounting (NCR 250–6000)

Electronic sales registers for the food service industry intended for use in high-volume restaurants and fast food service offer many innovations, and operators are able to establish tighter cash and inventory control while providing faster and more efficient customer service. Through the use of preset keys, automatic recording of prices without depressing numeric keys is possible. Item prices are stored in the memory of the machine and price charging is under management control. For example, if the price for chicken is set at £1·25 and stored in the memory of the machine, when the key for 'chicken' is depressed the machine

Fig. 10.9    NCR 250 electronic sales register (courtesy National Cash Register Co. Ltd.)

automatically adds £1·25 to the sale. Each item is given a code number—for example, apple tart is number 23; the operator depresses 23 on the numeric keys and the register automatically looks up the price and performs all the usual register functions. Automatic V.A.T. computation, change computation and coin dispensing are a feature of this machine. It can also supply detailed information on:

1. The number of customers served.
2. The number of portions sold of each item.
3. The net sales at any time of day.
4. The total of tax accountability.
5. Net sales and unit count for each department.
6. Automatically printed reports providing the information necessary to analyse the contribution of each menu item towards gross profit, which helps in the planning of additions to or deletions from the menu.
7. Print outs of various information for financial control reports: these reports simplify cash balancing, aid in maintaining control over credit transactions, and pinpoint sales activities.

# Guest accounting control systems (NCR 250)

Hotel accounting procedures are unique. Because payment is collected at check-out time, guests accounts must also be up to date and accurate. If the accounting system is inadequate, accounting errors will occur, causing financial loss or perhaps damage to the reputation of the hotel. Manufacturers have produced many sophisticated electronically controlled accounting systems offering better transaction control and more information for management control. Some of the features of these systems are:

1. *Multiple department keys.* These maintain separate totals for guest services which include, room charge, room service, restaurant service, bar service, valet, laundry, florist, garage and others. Itemised totals within revenue categories can be made available, for example revenue from room sales and revenue from restaurants.

2. *Multiple settlement keys.* A variety of keys provide separate totals for specific types of payment; whether the guest settles by cash, cheque, credit card or bank card, complete identification prints on the guest's bill and the journal.

3. *Cashier/shift responsibility.* A detailed record of cash and settlement responsibility by a cashier or shift is available. Cashier identification keys provide a separate report printed for each cashier. Resetting totals accommodate additional cashiers or shifts and a compulsory sign-in procedure ensures maximum cash control and prevents unauthorised use of the terminals. Cashier or shift identification is printed on all records.

4. *Cash sales.* A separate cash sales total for sundry items can be extracted and by allocating numeric codes separate sales totals for each item can be shown on revenue department reports. Itemised receipts enforce the recording of all sales.

5. *Room rates.* The machine is capable of storing room rates within its memory. The cashier enters the room rate code and presses the room rate key, and the terminal finds the rate for that room and prints the room charge on the bill. Room rates are under programme control and can only be changed by the management.

6. *Room number and balance pick-up.* Electronic check digit verification of room number and previous balance pick-up eliminate a common cause of error in posting to guests' bills. An automatic check digit is generated each time a new balance prints. Special room rates can be entered by using the room charge key.

7. *Telephone charges.* The rate for local or long distance calls can be preset and stored in the machine. The cashier simply enters the number of

calls made and depresses the preset telephone key and the total charge is automatically extended and printed on the guest's bill and on the journal.

8. *Paid out transactions.* Separate totals are available for paid out transactions affecting guests' accounts and hotel expense accounts.

9. *Control accounts.* Individual keys select advance reservation deposits, tabular ledger and cash sales. The guest account is automatically selected when the room number is entered. Cashiers must select the proper control prior to recording the transactions.

10. *V.A.T. calculations.* The total amount to be charged must be clearly indicated on the guest's statement at the time of collection. By using a pre-programmed percentage factor, calculation of Value Added Tax is automatic when the V.A.T. key is pressed. The total amount of tax prints but does not add to the balance if it is included in the various charges. If V.A.T. is not included in the charges, the total amount of tax due is calculated in the same manner, but is added to the balance figure.

11. *Advance payment transfer.* When the guest checks in, any advance payment is transferred from the advance reservations deposit account to the guest control account by using a credit balance pick-up key and advance payment transfer key.

12. *Ledger transfer.* Transfer from the guest control account to the ledger control account takes place automatically when the 'transfer to ledger' key is depressed. The amount is subtracted from one control account and added to the other in one simple operation.

13. *Error correction.* Posting errors are corrected by using the correction or void key on the machine. This assures management that all report totals are 'net', thus eliminating the need for time-consuming manual adjusting entries. Totals of all corrections are accumulated to retain complete management control.

14. *Package arrangements.* When certain services and accommodation are offered as a package or special-price arrangement, the machine can automatically distribute the charges and room rates to the respective revenue department totals. This information prints on the audit journal but only the total package price prints on the guest's account.

15. *Currency conversion.* For guests paying in foreign currency, the machine automatically converts one type of currency to another. The balance due in local currency is converted to foreign currency by dividing the balance amount by the conversion rate entered by the cashier. The entire transaction is recorded on a receipt.

16. *Service charge calculation.* Where a separate charge for service is to be added to the guest's bill, the charge is calculated and printed by depressing the service charge key, which uses a percentage factor store in the terminal. The service charge can be calculated each time

an item is posted or the terminal can be programmed to apply it against the balance at time of settlement.

17. *System reports.* The following reports illustrate the type of information which can be obtained from the system if the machine is so programmed.

18. *Cashier/shift report.* This report is a summary record of the individual settlement totals such as cash, cheques, credit cards, bankers cards. Separate totals are shown for Guests Paid Outs, House Paid Outs, Transfer to Ledger. Printed on the last line of the report is the cashier or shift number, date and consecutive transaction number.

19. *Cashiers' summary report.* This report is a consolidated listing of cash and settlement totals shown on individual cashier/shift reports. It summarises the activity of all cashiers and shows total sales, net amount paid after refunds, V.A.T. and total of guests' accounts transferred to the ledger control account.

20. *Guest account trial balance listing.* The trial balance listing indicates the room number and the current balance of each account and is produced automatically as part of the posting procedure.

21. *Guest account trial balance report.* This report summarises debit and credit balances of active and inactive guest accounts. The total is compared to the guest account control to prove the accuracy of the posting transaction. A trial balance report is taken also of advance reservation deposits and the ledger control account.

22. *Guest account control report.* This report reflects the net outstanding balance of the guest account ledger and summarises the debits, credits, transfers and settlements affecting the guests' accounts.

23. *Management control totals.* A total of daily group totals appearing on the cashiers' summary reports enables accountants and management to exercise strict control over all transactions.

24. *Revenue report.* This vital management report summarises all guest charges such as room charges, restaurant and bar service, room service charges, valet, laundry, telephone and other sundry sales. Guest charges can be attributed to individual areas, so that departmental individual totals are available.

# Progress test questions

1. What is the purpose of cash floats and how would you exercise control over them?
2. What method would you use to exercise control over sales through tills? Illustrate your answer with suitable diagrams of the returns required.

3. From the following information rule up and complete a suitable cashier's summary sheet. Service charge has to be calculated at $12\frac{1}{2}$% and Value Added Tax at 8%.

Cash bills (No cheques)

| Bill no. | No. of covers | Food £ | Drink £ |
|---|---|---|---|
| 3036 | 4 | 9·00 | 3·20 |
| 3045 | 2 | 4·50 | 1·35 |
| 3041 | 6 | 13·50 | 5·75 |
| 3037 | 4 | 9·00 | 1·65 |
| 3042 | 2 | 4·50 | 0·65 |
| 3046 | 3 | 6·75 | 2·20 |
| 3044 | 5 | 11·25 | 2·75 |
| 3048 | 2 | 4·50 | 0·80 |
| 3040 | 4 | 9·00 | 4·20 |

Credit bills

| | | | |
|---|---|---|---|
| 3038 Mr Brown Rm. 6 | 2 | 4·50 | 0·80 |
| 3039 Mr William Rm. 102 | 3 | 6·75 | 1·20 |
| 3043 Mr White Rm. 104 | 4 | 9·00 | 3·40 |
| 3047 Mrs Smith Rm. 9 | 4 | 9·00 | 2·90 |

4. When accepting cheques, of what must the cashier take particular note?
5. Explain two methods of controlling petty cash, illustrating your answer with a diagram.
6. What are the advantages of mechanised accounting?
7. Describe briefly some of the functions that can be performed by the latest electronic cash registers.
8. By what means can the modern electronic cash registers provide transaction control?
9. In the high-volume and fast-food-service industry, what valuable information can be provided by the use of modern electronic sales registers?
10. Describe some of the features of the latest guest accounting systems in use in the industry today.

# Part Three

# Budgetary Control

# CHAPTER 11

# Cost Concepts

## The nature and behaviour of costs

The costs incurred by a business consist of three basic elements, material cost, labour cost and overheads cost, and these elements also fall into three distinct groups from the point of view of their behaviour.

1. *Variable costs.* The food, drink, cigarettes and tobacco cost will vary and move usually in direct proportion to the volume of sales; for example, if food cost is calculated as a percentage of the sales, e.g. 38%:

$$\text{Food Cost} = \frac{38}{100} \text{ of £1,000 (Sales)} = £380$$

$$= \frac{38}{100} \text{ of £1,500 (Sales)} = £570$$

2. *Semi-variable costs.* Costs such as gas, electricity, fuel, breakages and cleaning materials will move with any variances in the volume of sales, but not in the same proportion; for example, if turnover increased by 10% the semi-variable cost would probably only increase approximately 1 or 2%.

3. *Fixed costs.* These costs, such as rent, rates, insurance, licences, depreciation, are usually fixed charges paid over a period of time, and will not vary with any change in the volume of sales.

For a business to be operated successfully it is necessary that costs be identified and the relationship between the volume of sales, the behaviour of the costs and what effect they have on the profitability of the business be appreciated; for example:

1. If the sales of a business increase 10%, the variable costs will increase in proportion, and the semi-variable costs will increase slightly, but the fixed costs will remain constant, and vice-versa if there is a decrease in sales.
2. Consideration of the figures in the following examples will show that the higher the proportion of fixed costs, the greater the effect an increase or decrease in sales will have on the net profit or loss of the business.

*Example 1:*

> *Restaurant A.* The sales figure for the period amounts to £2,000, the variable costs are £940, and the fixed costs £760:

| Restaurant A | | |
|---|---|---|
| | £ | |
| Variable costs | 940 | 47% |
| Fixed costs | 760 | 38% |
| Net profit | 300 | 15% |
| Sales | £2,000 | 100% |

A decrease of 10% in turnover will have the effect of a decrease in the variable costs, but the fixed costs will remain the same, with the following effect on Net Profit:

| Restaurant A | | |
|---|---|---|
| | £ | |
| Variable costs | 846 | 47·8% |
| Fixed costs | 760 | 42·2% |
| Net profit | 194 | 10·8% |
| Sales | £1,800 | 100·0% |

Consider *Restaurant B* with the same turnover of £2,000, but whose variable costs amount to £760, and fixed costs amount to £940:

| Restaurant B | | |
|---|---|---|
| | £ | |
| Variable costs | 760 | 38% |
| Fixed costs | 940 | 47% |
| Net profit | 300 | 15% |
| Sales | £2,000 | 100% |

Note the effect on the percentage of fixed costs and net profit if there is the same decrease of 10% in sales:

| Restaurant B | | |
|---|---|---|
| | £ | |
| Variable costs | 684 | 38·0% |
| Fixed costs | 940 | 52·2% |
| Net profit | 176 | 9·8% |
| Sales | £1,800 | 100·0% |

*Conclusion: Restaurant A*—A decrease of 10% in sales resulted in an increase of 4·2% for fixed costs and a decrease of 4·2% in net profit.

*Restaurant B*—A decrease of 10% of this restaurant's turnover, with higher fixed costs, resulted in an increase of 5·2% for fixed costs and a decrease of 5·2% in net profit.

*Example 2:*
    Consider the same two restaurants if there is an *increase* of 10% in sales:

|  | Restaurant A £ | Restaurant A % | Restaurant B £ | Restaurant B % |
|---|---|---|---|---|
| Variable costs | 1,034 | 47·0 | 836 | 38·0 |
| Fixed costs | 760 | 34·6 | 940 | 42·7 |
| Net profit | 406 | 18·4 | 424 | 19·3 |
| Sales | £2,200 | 100·0% | £2,200 | 100·0% |

*Conclusion: Restaurant A*—An increase of 10% in sales resulted in a decrease of 3·4% in fixed costs and an increase of 3·4% in net profit.

*Restaurant B*—An increase of 10% in sales resulted in a decrease of 4·3% in fixed costs and an increase of 4·3% in net profit.

When turnover decreases the restaurant with the higher percentage of fixed costs will show the greater percentage decrease in net profit and when turnover increases the net profit tends to increase more in proportion.

# Unit costs

By analysing the costs for each unit sold, it is possible to see the effect an increase in sales will have on the net profit or loss made by each unit.

*Example 3:*
    A restaurant serves between 700 and 1,000 meals per week. A meal is sold in the restaurant for £2·20 (V.A.T. exclusive). The food cost is 40% of the selling price. The fixed costs for the restaurant amount to £966 per week. The variable costs of each meal amount to:

$$\frac{40}{100} \times £2 \cdot 20 = 88p$$

The fixed cost of £966 is divided by the number of meals served; therefore the greater the number of meals served, the smaller the amount of fixed cost attributed to each meal.

| Selling price per meal £2·20 | Number of meals served | | | |
|---|---|---|---|---|
| | 700 | 800 | 900 | 1,000 |
| | £ | £ | £ | £ |
| Variable cost per meal | 0·88 | 0·88 | 0·88 | 0·88 |
| Fixed cost per meal | 1·38 | 1·2075 | 1·073 | 0·966 |
| Total cost per meal | 2·26 | 2·0875 | 1·953 | 1·846 |
| Net profit per meal (+) | — | +0·1125 | +0·247 | +0·354 |
| Net loss per meal (−) | −0·06 | — | — | — |

Fig. 11.1   Unit profit/loss per meal

*Conclusion:* The restaurant will make a loss if it serves less than 750 meals. If fixed costs remain constant per week the more meals served the greater the net profit per meal.

# Break-even point

It is important that management are aware what level of turnover is necessary to cover all costs, and at what point a profit will start being made. This is called the 'break-even point' and can be illustrated by means of a tabular statement or by presenting the information in a graph form. To construct a break-even chart or statement for a restaurant, the following information is required:

1. *The number of customers per week.* This can be ascertained from the cashier's analysis sheet, which shows the total number of covers as extracted from the customers' bills.

2. *The average spending power of the customer.* This can be ascertained by dividing the total sales by the number of customers served.

3. *Fixed costs.* The annual expenses such as rent, rates, insurance, depreciation, wages, salaries, etc., can be divided by 52 to ascertain the average fixed costs per week.

4. *Variable costs.* Food, drink, tobacco and other variable costs are usually calculated as a percentage of the sales figure.

*Example 4:*
    The Flamingo Restaurant serves between 600 and 1,000 customers per week. The average spending power per customer is £2·50. The food cost is estimated at 38% of the sales. The fixed costs amount to £990 per week which will include the average labour cost per week.

1. The sales figure is calculated by multiplying the average spending power by the number of customers.
2. The variable costs are calculated by finding 38% of the sales figure.
3. The fixed costs of £990 remain constant.

*The Flamingo Restaurant*
*Break-even point*

| Number of customers | Total sales | Variable costs | Fixed costs | Total costs | Net profit (+) | Net loss (−) | % | Break-even point |
|---|---|---|---|---|---|---|---|---|
| | £ | £ | £ | £ | £ | £ | | |
| 600 | 1,500 | 570 | 990 | 1,560 | | −60 | −0·4 | * |
| 700 | 1,750 | 665 | 990 | 1,655 | +95 | | +5·4 | |
| 800 | 2,000 | 760 | 990 | 1,750 | +250 | | +12·5 | |
| 900 | 2,250 | 855 | 990 | 1,845 | +405 | | +18·0 | |
| 1,000 | 2,500 | 950 | 990 | 1,940 | +560 | | +26·0 | |

Fig. 11.2  Break-even analysis: tabular solution

Fig. 11.3  Break-even analysis: graphical solution

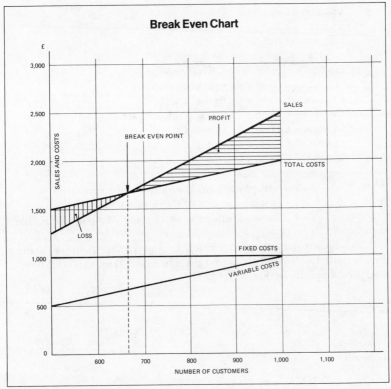

*Conclusion:*

(a) The restaurant would have to serve at least 650 customers in order to break-even.

(b) If fixed costs remain constant, every increase of 100 customers increases the net profit of the restaurant by £155.

(c) The increase in sales results in a net profit increase more than in proportion.

Break-even charts can also be prepared to ascertain the break-even point and the volume of sales necessary to produce a required profit.

*Example 5:*

A restaurant has semi-variable expenses and labour costs which amount to an estimated 28% of the sales; the fixed expenses amount to £2,640 p.a. and management requires a 65% gross profit margin:

To prepare the graph

1. Find 65% of:
   £5,000 = £3,250
   £10,000 = £6,500
   £15,000 = £9,750
   £20,000 = £13,000
   £25,000 = £16,250
   £30,000 = £19,500

2. Find 28% of:          plus fixed expenses
   £5,000 = £1,400 + £2,640 = £4,040
   £10,000 = £2,800 + £2,640 = £5,440
   £15,000 = £4,200 + £2,640 = £6,840
   £20,000 = £5,600 + £2,640 = £8,240
   £25,000 = £7,000 + £2,640 = £9,640
   £30,000 = £8,400 + £2,640 = £11,040

When these figures are plotted on the graph the break-even point is approximately £7,300 sales, i.e. 65% of £7,300 = £4,745.

Semi-variable + Labour cost = 28% of £7,300 = £2,044, plus fixed expenses £2,640 = £4,684.

Which means that when sales reach £7,300 management will achieve their required 65% gross profit margin. The graph (Fig. 11.4) can then be interpreted as follows (Fig. 11.5).

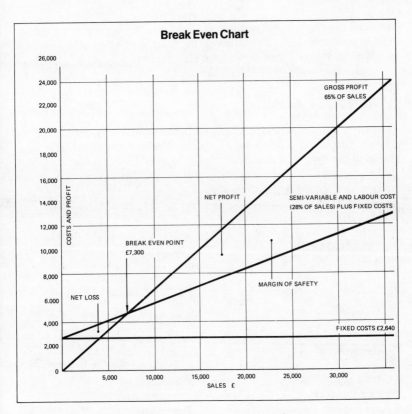

Fig. 11.4 Volume of sales required to produce a given net profit

Fig. 11.5 Interpretation of Fig. 11.4

| Sales | 65% Gross profit on sales | Semi-variable labour and fixed costs | Net loss (−) | Net profit (+) | Profit increase per £5,000 turnover |
|---|---|---|---|---|---|
| £ | £ | £ | £ | £ | £ |
| 5,000 | 3,250 | 4,040 | 790 | — | — |
| 10,000 | 6,500 | 5,440 | — | 1,060 | (1,850) |
| 15,000 | 9,750 | 6,840 | — | 2,910 | 1,850 |
| 20,000 | 13,000 | 8,240 | — | 4,760 | 1,850 |
| 25,000 | 16,250 | 9,640 | — | 6,610 | 1,850 |
| 30,000 | 19,500 | 11,040 | — | 8,460 | 1,850 |

By studying the graph it will be noted that as the range between sales and total cost widens the margin of safety widens, which means that a considerable decrease in the sales volume is possible before the business incurs a loss; however, when the range is narrow, even a small decrease in sales can convert any net profit into a loss. The higher the ratio of fixed costs to variable costs, the narrower the margin of safety; the lower the ratio of fixed costs, the wider the margin of safety.

# Marginal cost

When a business is seasonal, whether or not it should remain open during the off-season could depend on the ratio of fixed costs to variable costs, for to break even the sales must cover the fixed costs and variable costs and as the sales could drop considerably during the off season, a narrow margin of safety could result in a loss.

*Example 6:*

The following information was extracted from the books of a seasonal hotel:

| *On-season* 1 April–30 September | £ | *Off-season* 1 October–31 March | £ |
|---|---|---|---|
| Net sales | 35,000 | Net sales | 15,000 |
| *Less* Cost of sales | 13,300 | *Less* Cost of sales | 5,700 |
| Gross profit | 21,700 | Gross profit | 9,300 |
| | | | |
| Wages and salaries | 10,500 | Wages and salaries | 5,500 |
| Rates, insurance | 1,750 | Rates, insurance | 1,750 |
| Depreciation | 1,500 | Depreciation | 1,500 |
| Gas and electricity | 800 | Gas and electricity | 950 |
| Cleaning materials | 500 | Cleaning materials | 300 |
| Laundry | 400 | Laundry | 250 |
| Postage and stationery | 200 | Postage and stationery | 150 |
| Advertising | 400 | Advertising | 200 |
| Telephone | 250 | Telephone | 200 |
| Sundry expenses | 150 | Sundry expenses | 100 |
| | £16,560 | | £10,900 |
| Net profit | £5,250 | Net loss | £1,600 |

If the hotel closed during the off-season, the fixed expenses would still have to be paid; these are:

|                                              | £       |
| -------------------------------------------- | ------- |
| Rates and insurance                          | 1,750   |
| Depreciation (half usual when equipment not in use) | 750 |
|                                              | £2,500  |

Therefore the hotel would be £2,500−£1,600=£900 worse off if it closed. The effect on the net profit if the hotel closed would be as follows:

| Expenses saved:          | £       |
| ------------------------ | ------- |
| Wages and salaries       | 5,500   |
| Depreciation (half)      | 750     |
| Gas and electricity      | 950     |
| Cleaning materials       | 300     |
| Laundry                  | 250     |
| Postage and stationery   | 150     |
| Advertising              | 200     |
| Telephone                | 200     |
| Sundry expenses          | 100     |
|                          | £8,400  |

|                                  | £       |
| -------------------------------- | ------- |
| Loss of income (gross profit)    | 9,300   |
| Less Savings of expenses         | 8,400   |
| Hotel worse off by               | £900    |

When deciding whether to close during the off-season, the hotelier would have to take into consideration the following factors:

1. Would the net loss be reduced?
2. Would the total net profit for the year be increased?
3. Would the existing experienced staff be available at the beginning of the new season?
4. Would it be worth considering offering special reduced rates to parties during the off-season in order to gain additional income, to offset against costs?

# Apportionment of costs

The functions of a hotel are divided into three activities, the provision of accommodation, the sale of food and the sale of liquor and tobacco; and the cost of labour and expenses should be directly attributed to each particular activity so that the profitability of each can be examined separately and action taken by management when required.

It is a simple matter to allocate direct labour and direct expenses to the source of income: wages for kitchen and waiting staff to the restaurant, bar staff to bars, housekeepers and chambermaids to accommodation. Similarly, certain expenses can be identified specifically with restaurant, bars and accommodation. Wages for staff that service the hotel as a whole, such as management, front office staff, porters and maintenance will need to be apportioned between each activity, as will the other expenses which are attributable to all departments. A simple method of apportioning these indirect labour costs and expenses is by dividing them in proportion to the sales from each source:

*Example 7:*
Total net sales of a hotel were:

|  | £ |
|---|---|
| Accommodation | 23,000 |
| Meals | 16,000 |
| Bars | 3,000 |
|  | £42,000 |

The direct labour and expenses have been allocated to their respective departments and £2,700 wages and £4,100 overheads have to be apportioned between the three sections in proportion to their sales.

The total expenses are multipled by the sales of the department and divided by the total sales of the hotel:

|  | *Wages* | *Overheads* |
|---|---|---|
| Accommodation | $\frac{£2,700 \times £23,000}{£42,000} = £1,478$ | $\frac{£4,100 \times £23,000}{£42,000} = £2,245$ |
| Meals | $\frac{£2,700 \times £16,000}{£42,000} = £1,029$ | $\frac{£4,100 \times £16,000}{£42,000} = £1,562$ |
| Bars | $\frac{£2,700 \times £3,000}{£42,000} = £193$ | $\frac{£4,100 \times £3,000}{£42,000} = £293$ |

Another method of apportioning the expenses attributable to the whole hotel is by estimating the floor area actually used by each department and charging the expenses in proportion. By this method the amount charged to each department will not be affected by any fluctuation in turnover.

*Example 8:*
The total floor area of a hotel which includes bedrooms, restaurants, bars and public rooms amounts to 25,000 square metres, of which 3,000 square metres are public lounges or service areas.

The relative floor areas to be proportioned are:

|                | $m^2$  | % of total |
| -------------- | ------ | ---------- |
| Accommodation  | 16,060 | 73         |
| Restaurant     | 4,840  | 22         |
| Bars           | 1,100  | 5          |
|                | 22,000 | 100%       |

Direct labour and expenses have been allocated to the source of income and every month £3,200 wages and £5,400 overheads have to be apportioned on a floor area basis.

*Wages*
£

Accommodation $\dfrac{73}{100} \times \dfrac{£3,200}{1} =$ 2,336

Restaurant $\dfrac{22}{100} \times \dfrac{£3,200}{1} =$ 704

Bars $\dfrac{5}{100} \times \dfrac{£3,200}{1} =$ 160

£3,200

*Overheads*
£

Accommodation $\dfrac{73}{100} \times \dfrac{£5,400}{1} =$ 3,942

Restaurant $\dfrac{22}{100} \times \dfrac{£5,400}{1} =$ 1,188

Bars $\dfrac{5}{100} \times \dfrac{£5,400}{1} =$ 270

£5,400

## Meter consumption control

Control can be exercised over the water, gas and electricity consumption of each department by installing separate meters; thus the cost becomes a direct expense as opposed to being an indirect expense. The amounts used by the areas servicing the whole department are the only expense that will have to be apportioned to all departments.

## Calculation of charges

In order to plan a scale of charges necessary to cover all costs and provide a reasonable return on capital invested, the hotelier would need to ascertain the following:

1. The estimated number of guests per week, or the rate of guest occupancy, which is the number of guests staying in the hotel in relation to the guest capacity of the hotel.

*Example 9:*
    A 60-bedroomed hotel can accommodate 100 guests when full. One week of full occupancy would therefore be $100 \times 7$ nights $= 700$ sleeper nights. If 30 double rooms and 12 single rooms are occupied during the week, that would be $72 \times 7 = 504$ sleeper nights. Rate of room occupancy:

$$\frac{\text{Actual number of guests}}{\text{Guest capacity}} = \frac{504}{700} \times \frac{100}{1} = 72\%$$

As a basis for fixing charges one would have to calculate the overall seasonal or yearly average room occupancy, either as a percentage or number of guests.

2. The type of menu to be offered would be costed and the average food cost allowance per head per week would be estimated.
3. The average labour cost including the cost of any staff meals and accommodation would be calculated and the weekly average would be estimated.
4. The average overheads cost per annum, including depreciation and any interest on capital investment that has to be provided for, would be calculated and an estimated weekly cost ascertained.
5. The minimum net profit percentage required would be decided by management.

*Example 10:*
    A small hotel with 25 double bedrooms and 10 singles has a guest capacity of 60 guests. It has been anticipated that an average 60% guest occupancy can be expected. Specimen menus have been costed for inclusive meals and the estimated food cost will amount to £13·30 per guest per week. Labour costs, which include staff meals and accommodation, are estimated at £19,650 per annum. Overheads are estimated at £8,340 per annum. Interest on capital invested of £40,000 must be allowed for at 7% per annum, and it is desired to make a minimum net profit of 15% per annum.

*Solution:*
Guest occupancy 60% of guest capacity of 60

$$= \frac{60}{100} \times \frac{60}{1} = 36 \text{ guests per week.}$$

| *Food cost* | | £ |
|---|---|---|
| 36 guests for 52 weeks at £13·30 per guest per week = £24,897·60 | say | 24,900 |
| *Labour cost* | | 19,650 |
| *Overheads* | | 8,340 |
| *Interest on capital* (7% p.a. on £40,000) | | 2,800 |
| | | £55,690 |

If a net profit of 15% of sales is required, the food cost, labour cost, overheads and interest on capital will represent 85% of sales, therefore:

$$\frac{£55,690}{85} = 1\%$$

$$\frac{£55,690}{85} \times 100 = 100\%, \text{ which is the sales figure}$$

$$= £65,518·00 \quad \text{say } £65,520·00$$

Net profit (15% of £65,520) will be £9,830

*Statement of estimated costs*

| | £ | % of Sales |
|---|---|---|
| Food cost | 24,900 | 38·0 |
| Labour cost | 19,650 | 30·0 |
| Overheads | 8,340 | 12·6 |
| Interest on capital | 2,800 | 4·4 |
| Net profit | 9,830 | 15·0 |
| Sales required to cover costs: | £65,520 | 100·0% |

Estimated number of guests per annum: $36 \times 52 = 1,872$ p.a.

Average charge per week: $\dfrac{£65,520}{1,872} = £35$ per week

If the inclusive charge for accommodation, breakfast, lunch and dinner is £35 per week and food cost is £13·30 per week, the amount allocated to accommodation is £21·70.

Therefore: $\dfrac{£21·70}{7} = £3·10$ per sleeper night

To calculate charges for meals to chance guests:

$$\frac{£13·30}{7} = £1·90 \text{ per day food cost}$$

| | £ | |
|---|---|---|
| Say | 0·30 is allowed for breakfast | |
| | 0·70 is allowed for lunch | |
| | 0·90 is allowed for dinner | |
| | £1·90 Total food cost | |

As the establishment requires a 62% gross profit margin

$$(\text{Sales} - \text{Food cost} = \text{Gross profit})$$
$$100\% \qquad 38\% \qquad 62\%$$

The *minimum* charge would be:

Breakfast $\dfrac{30p \times 100}{38} = 79p$ (say 80p)

Lunch $\dfrac{70p \times 100}{38} = £1·84$ (say £1·85)

Dinner $\dfrac{90p \times 100}{38} = £2·37$ (say £2·40)

Therefore a minimum charge for bed and breakfast would be:

| | £ |
|---|---|
| Accommodation: | 3·10 |
| Breakfast: | 0·80 |
| | £3·90 |

It must be remembered that the calculation of charges based on the variable and fixed costs of an establishment serve as a guide to the minimum charges possible if all costs are to be recovered and the required net profit is to be achieved. The actual tariff, restaurant or bar charges will be decided by management after consideration of demand and a study of immediate competitors' prices for the same standards of accommodation and service; for in the ultimate it is what the customer is prepared to pay that is the deciding factor.

# Progress test questions

1. Explain what you understand by:

   (a) Variable costs:
   (b) Semi-variable costs; and
   (c) Fixed costs.

2. (a) From the following information prepare a statement showing the net profit, expressing each cost and the net profit as a percentage of sales, for the Jarra Restaurant for the year ended 31 December, 19 . .

   Variable costs (food, drink, tobacco) £12,600; Fixed costs (rent, rates, insurance, etc.) £10,800; Semi-variable costs (light, heat, telephone, etc.) £9,000; Sales £36,000.

   (b) It is estimated that the sales will increase by 10% next year, fixed costs will remain constant, the variable cost percentage will be in the same ratio to sales, and the semi-variable costs will increase by 2%. Prepare a statement showing the effect on the net profit and other costs and percentages.

3. From the following information prepare a unit cost, profit/loss statement:

   The Mary-Ann Restaurant serves between 500 and 800 meals per week. The average price spent by the customers is £1·25 per meal. The variable costs (food cost) is 42p per meal, and the fixed costs amount to £450 per week.

4. (a) Prepare a break-even tabular statement and break-even chart from the following information.

   The Regina Restaurant serves between 1,300 and 1,700 customers per week. The average customer spending is £1·25, the fixed costs are £875 per week and the variable costs (food, drink, etc.) amount to 45% of sales.

   (b) Comment on your findings.

5. The St. Peter's Hotel is a seasonal establishment and the following analysis of trading was prepared:

| | April–September £ | October–March £ |
|---|---|---|
| Net sales | 22,000 | 12,000 |
| Cost of sales | 7,920 | 4,200 |
| Wages and salaries | 6,219 | 4,360 |
| Rates and insurance (fixed cost) | 1,500 | 1,500 |
| Depreciation (fixed cost) | 1,200 | 1,200 |
| Heat and light | 750 | 1,050 |
| Cleaning materials, breakages, postage and stationery, telephone, sundry expenses, etc. | 1,814 | 1,540 |

   (a) Prepare a statement showing the gross profit and net profit achieved for the on-season and off-season.

   (b) From your findings, comment on whether you would recommend that the hotel close during the off-season, giving your reasons.

6. The net sales of a hotel for the trading period were: rooms £18,000, meals £11,000, bars £2,000. Indirect wages amount to £820 and general overhead expenses to £1,250. Apportion these expenses between the three departments in the ratio of their sales.

7. The total floor area of an hotel amounts to 15,000 m², of which 2,000 m² are public rooms and service areas. The other relative areas are: rooms 9,500 m²; restaurant 2,600 m²; bars 900 m². Direct labour and direct expenses have been allocated to their respective departments. Apportion the indirect wages £1,400, and general overheads £2,200 on a floor area basis.

8. The Horizon Hotel has 30 double rooms and 15 singles, and opens for a season of 36 weeks. It is estimated that there will be an overall average guest occupancy of 60% of the guest capacity. Wages for staff including staff meals are estimated at £14,580, and overheads are estimated at £9,620. Interest on capital investment £25,000 has to be provided for at 7% p.a. The variable cost (food cost) is estimated at £12·80 per guest per week for inclusive meals. Management wish to make a net profit of 10%.

   (a) Calculate the average charge per guest per week (to the nearest £) necessary to cover costs and profit.
   (b) If the food cost for breakfast is 35p, lunch 60p, dinner 80p, calculate meal charges to chance guests if management require a 60% gross profit margin.
   (c) Recommend a minimum charge for bed and breakfast.

# CHAPTER 12

# Budgetary Control

## Objects and advantages

A budget is primarily a projected plan expressed in financial or other terms which sets the objectives of the business and provides a means of control by the measurement of the actual results against the plan.

A fundamental of budgetary control is that the responsibility for the various budgets is assigned to the respective managers. A continual comparison of actual results with the budgets is made and when variances occur they are examined, and the causes determined. It is essential that any corrective action necessary is taken immediately because of the effect it may have on the profitability of the business.

### *Advantages*

The main advantages of budgetary control can be summarised as follows:

1. The budget is a detailed plan and provides the means of regulating the progress of the business.
2. The budget sets standards of performance which can be measured and assessed.
3. Budgetary control establishes clear lines of responsibility and co-ordinates all activities.
4. It ensures the best possible use of resources and helps maximise profits.
5. It controls expenditure and promotes cost-consciousness and cost responsibility within the departments.
6. The budget sets targets for the various managers and budgetary control helps to ensure that the objectives are achieved.

## The budget committee

When an organisation decides to implement a system of budgetary control, it is usual to constitute a budget committee. This committee normally includes the managing director or general manager, the food and beverage controller, the head chef, the head housekeeper, the banqueting manager and the senior accountant.

The main functions of the committee are to decide:

1. What system of budgetary control is most suitable for the structure of their particular organisation;
2. The authority and responsibility of each manager;
3. Budget proposals in draft form for submission to the Board of Directors.

## Formulation of budgets

Before budgets can be prepared it is necessary to have the maximum available information and data on the following:

1. Full details of past performance, which entails complete analysis of sales and expenditure. This information is obtainable from the accounts.
2. A study of the current trends of sales, the sales mix, advance bookings, special function business.
3. Other information such as the state of employment, condition and prosperity of local industry, the political situation, future developments and their likely effect on turnover and expenses, and the services offered and prices charged by competitors.

# The budget period

The formulation of a budget presupposes that it will relate to a period of time. In general the appropriate budget periods for a hotel are a year, and each month of the year, the total of the monthly estimates being the annual estimate. The budget for the year gives the overall planned results, the breakdown will show the contribution made each month, providing a basis for continual comparison. In seasonal hotels there will emerge a fairly definite cycle of activity covering one year and this will be translated into terms of seasonal objectives. As months have slightly different numbers of days and end on different days of the week, calendar months may be unsatisfactory units of time when comparisons have to be made. There are two different methods of dividing the year for budgeting purposes.

## Method 1

The year is divided into 12 accounting periods, each quarter consisting of two four-week and one five-week period (13 weeks). Not all months within the year will be comparable in length, but each month can be compared with the same month in the previous year, and each quarter will cover 13 weeks.

# Method 2

The year is divided into 13 accounting periods so that every month can be compared with every other month. The month would end on different days, but this method is more advantageous for comparisons and estimating.

*Example 1:*

| Period | 4 weeks: |
|--------|----------|
| 1 | January 1–January 28 |
| 2 | January 29–February 25 |
| 3 | February 26–March 25 |
| 4 | March 26–April 22 |
| 5 | April 23–May 20 |
| 6 | May 21–June 17 |
| 7 | June 18–July 15 |
| 8 | July 16–August 12 |
| 9 | August 13–September 9 |
| 10 | September 10–October 7 |
| 11 | October 8–November 4 |
| 12 | November 5–December 2 |
| 13 | December 3–December 31 |

# Types of budgets

There are two main classifications of budgets—capital budgets, which are concerned with the assets and liabilities of the business, and revenue budgets, which are concerned with income, expenses and profits. These are divided into operating budgets dealing with sales, purchases, office and administration expenses, labour costs, maintenance costs, etc.

There are also two main means of preparing budgets to control expenditure.

## 1. Fixed budgets

These budgets have fixed amounts allocated for expenditure before the commencement of the budget period. For example, advertising, printing, stationery, office expenses are each allocated a fixed sum, and expenditure on these items must be kept within the limits of the budget set.

## 2. Flexible budgets

As the term implies, expenditure in these budgets is predetermined as a proportion of the level of sales and must therefore be 'flexible'. For example, in a seasonal establishment the labour budget would be 'flexible', for the labour costs during the 'on-season' will vary considerably to that for the 'off-season', as will various budgeted overhead and raw material costs.

# Development of budgets

The ultimate object of budgeting is to develop an overall profit budget for the business. In the process of development, separate budgets will be prepared for the component items of income and expenditure, for example:

Sales
Purchases
Other income
Expenses
Labour costs
Maintenance costs

The information from these functional budgets is used to prepare departmental budgets, and from these, the budgeted results are consolidated into the preparation of master budgets controlling the overall operations of the hotel as a whole.

## Sales

A realistic sales budget can be prepared for each revenue producing department after taking into consideration the following factors:

(a) The special circumstances affecting each department;
(b) Complete analysis of the previous year's actual sales figures for each department;
(c) An analysis of the sales mix percentages;
(d) A careful study of probable future trends.

## Purchases

If the establishment is working on a fixed food and beverage cost percentage, then it is a simple matter to apply this percentage to the budgeted sales and prepare a purchases budget, but careful attention must be paid to the following:

(a) Any significant change in the sales mix must be analysed to see what effect it will have on the purchases budget.

(b) Any change in the use of food stuffs, e.g. convenience and pre-packed commodities must be noted and studied for effect on the cost of purchases.

(c) Any change in suppliers may affect costs.

(d) Prices must be under constant surveillance.

## Other income

The income expected from other activities such as special functions, vending machines, sporting facilities, garaging, and valeting business will be budgeted in the same manner as for usual sales, but with the costs of each item related to the anticipated income from these sources.

## Expenses

Budgets for the various overhead expenses will use the figures or percentages of the previous year as a basis. Fixed expenses such as rent, rates, insurance and depreciation can be forecast with a degree of accuracy, but variable expenses must be estimated after consideration of any known or anticipated increase in charges expected for such items as gas, electricity, fuel, etc.

## Labour costs

The labour cost budget will use the labour cost percentage of sales for the previous year as its basis for preparation, then take the following factors into consideration:

(a) Any anticipated change in wage levels;

(b) The number of staff needed to meet requirements;

(c) Any changes anticipated in the grading of staff;

(d) Any statutory changes expected in National Insurance contributions.

## Maintenance

These budgets are normally 'fixed' and are dependent on finance available for such projects as painting, decorating and regular maintenance of equipment on a contract basis. Other expenditure for repairs and maintenance are usually budgeted on the basis of expenditure of the previous year, allowing for any normal price increases expected.

## Departmental budgets

Once the overall picture of sales, purchases, other income, expenses, labour costs and maintenance has been established, it is comparatively simple to prepare budgets and set targets for each department. Direct expenses and labour costs can be attributed to the appropriate department, and indirect expenses and labour can be apportioned to each department by the methods discussed in Chapter 11.

## Master budgets

By summarising the information of all the departmental budgets, a master profit plan for all the activity centres of the hotel can be prepared for the budget period. Continuous departmental and overall comparisons of budgeted against actual results are an effective method of exercising control over the whole operation.

# Limiting factors

In the preparation of budgets the most important step is to forecast and set targets for the future volume of sales; therefore any factor that will obstruct or limit any further increase in sales must be identified, investigated and, if possible, eliminated before any progress can be made in the preparation of budgets. This limiting factor is often referred to as the 'key factor', 'governing factor' or 'principal budget factor', and in the hotel and catering industry the limiting factors which can prevent further increase in sales can be identified as follows.

## 1. Size and capacity of the establishment

In hotels, motels and other establishments which provide accommodation, the maximum occupancy will be controlled by the number of rooms available for letting. Once maximum occupancy has been attained, there can be no further increase in the volume sales from that source unless prices are increased or there are extensions to the premises providing more rooms for letting.

## 2. Special functions capacity

The volume of sales from special function business will be limited by the availability of facilities. The hotel will only be able to accept bookings in accordance with the accommodation and facilities they are able to provide.

## 3. Seating capacity

Restaurants are only able to accommodate the number of customers for which they have seats available, so that once the restaurant is full to capacity and the average spending power per customer has reached the maximum for the type of service offered, then any increase in sales would only be achieved by quicker turnround, an increase in prices or extension to the restaurant to make more seats available.

## 4. Consumer demand

This is the most difficult limiting factor to resolve, for consumer demand can be dependent on so many other factors, for example, the area, population, average income of the people in the catchment area, prosperity of local industry, transport facilities, the weather, number of competitors and their prices. When consumer demand has reached its peak only careful market research will pinpoint ways and means of increasing demand and thus increasing potential sales.

## 5. Quality of management and labour

Good quality management and staff will enhance the reputation of the establishment and thus increase the sales potential, while poor quality executives and staff will be a definite limiting factor, for inefficient, untrained and unskilled staff can have a disastrous effect on the sales potential of an establishment. The skill of the chef and kitchen staff will be reflected in the quality of food served and the efficiency of the waiting staff will be reflected in the service given.

A shortage of good quality executives will result in bad organisation and many opportunities to increase sales could be lost through inefficient and unimaginative management.

## 6. Insufficient capital

A business could possibly increase the volume of sales by extensions to premises or the acquisition of further units, but if there is insufficient capital available to carry out such projects, then there is a positive limiting factor.

## 7. Management policy

If the management have laid down a set policy that it will only cater for a certain type of customer and will not accept certain types of business such as coach parties, football or rugby team functions, or package tour holidaymakers, then the management's policy itself could prove to be a limiting factor. Once the maximum sales from business based on the lines laid down by management policy have been realised, only a change in policy will effect an increase in sales.

# Pricing policy

Too many hoteliers and caterers attempt to offset the price rises in food, drink and other commodities and services by simply passing on these increases to the consumer. This is not always a wise policy, for it must be remembered that the consumer may also be on a planned budget and when he reaches his maximum spending limit on items such as having a meal out, or the type of accommodation he is able to afford, the deciding factor may be the prices charged by the restaurant or the hotel. Once the establishment exceeds the limit of its customers' spending power, the customers will go elsewhere, resulting in loss of business to the establishment.

It is often a wiser policy when confronted by price rises for the hotelier or caterer to look for ways and means of absorbing some of them by making his establishment function more efficiently and ensuring no wastage. Whenever possible the caterer should try and keep his charges reasonably stable.

# Progress test questions

1. What are the objects and advantages of budgetary control?

2. What is the function of the budget committee?

3. Explain two methods of defining the budget period.

4. What do you understand by a 'fixed budget' and a 'flexible budget'?

5. Write brief notes on the factors to be considered when preparing budgets for the following:

   (a) Sales
   (b) Purchases
   (c) Expenses
   (d) Labour costs
   (e) Maintenance.

6. What do you understand by the term 'limiting factor'? Give examples.

7. What factors must be considered when deciding on a pricing policy?

# CHAPTER 13

# Financial Budgets

## Profits budgets

It is difficult to forecast the profitability of a business when no previous figures exist, as in a new business. In such a case all known facts must be taken into account and maximum information obtained about similar types of establishment offering the same kind of service in the same location. This information can be used as a guide for estimating. The starting point is to estimate the maximum possible sales for the budget period.

Restaurants can get at this figure by knowing the number of seats available, and the average amount spent by the customers, and the rate of seat occupancy. The use of ratios provide management with a measure and data on which to review progress, and the following operating statistics will assist in the interpretation of the trend of profitability.

## *Rate of seat occupancy*

This is usually calculated as a percentage by relating the number of meals served to the seating capacity of the restaurant.

Seating capacity             120
Number of meals served        84

$$\text{then } \frac{84}{120} \times \frac{100}{1} = 70\% \text{ seat occupancy}$$

If the same restaurant serves lunch and dinner the total daily seating capacity would be 240, and if on a particular day 360 meals were served the rate of seat occupancy is:

$$\frac{\text{Meals served}}{\text{Seating capacity}} = \frac{360}{240} = 1 \cdot 5 \text{ ratio} (150\%)$$

The ratio of $1 \cdot 5$ shows that the average seat available was relaid $1 \cdot 5$ times. The higher the rate the more economical the use being made of the restaurant equipment and facilities.

# Average spending power

The total sales of a business will depend on the number of customers and the average amount spent per customer. Average spending power is calculated by dividing the total sales by the number of meals served or number of customers:

$$\frac{\text{Sales}}{\text{Number of meals served}} = \frac{£810}{360} = £2 \cdot 25 \text{ average}$$

A study over a few weeks of the average seat occupancy, average number of customers and average takings, plus careful market research on similar types of establishments will make it possible to do a customer projection chart and thus arrive at a fairly accurate prediction of potential turnover for the year.

Fig. 13.1   Customer projection chart

---

Maximum seating capacity: 240
Average spending power: £2·25

| | % | No. of customers | £ |
|---|---|---|---|
| Monday | 58 | 139 | 312·75 |
| Tuesday | 56 | 135 | 303·75 |
| Wednesday | 57 | 137 | 308·25 |
| Thursday | 64 | 154 | 346·50 |
| Friday | 85 | 204 | 459·00 |
| Saturday | 100 | 240 | 540·00 |
| Weekly totals: | 420 | 1,009 | 2,270·25 |

*Analysis:* Average seat occupancy: $\dfrac{\text{Total of percentages}}{\text{No. of days}}$ $\dfrac{420}{6} = 70\%$

Average no. of customers: $\dfrac{1,009}{6} = 168$

Average takings: $\dfrac{£2,270}{6} = £378$

---

To estimate the average yearly turnover:

52 weeks × £2,270 = £118,040

# Preparation of profits budget

If the budget period is divided into 13 accounting periods, the estimated turnover for one accounting period will be:

$$\frac{£118,040}{13} = £9,080$$

If management have decided they require a 65% gross profit margin to cover labour costs, fixed and variable overhead costs, and provide a reasonable net profit and the estimated labour costs are £2,724, the fixed costs (rent, rates, insurance and depreciation) are £1,544, and the variable overhead costs are £726, an estimated profit budget can be prepared as follows:

Fig. 13.2   Estimated profit budget (monthly)

| | Period 1: Jan. 1–28 | | | | Period 2: Jan. 29–Feb. 28 | | | | Period 3: Feb 28–Mar. 25 | | | |
|---|---|---|---|---|---|---|---|---|---|---|---|---|
| | Budget | | Actual | | Budget | | Actual | | Budget | | Actual | |
| | £ | % | £ | % | £ | % | £ | % | £ | % | £ | % |
| Sales | 9,080 | 100 | | | 9,080 | 100 | | | 9,080 | 100 | | |
| Cost of sales | 3,178 | 35 | | | 3,178 | 35 | | | 3,178 | 35 | | |
| Gross profit | 5,902 | 65 | | | 5,902 | 65 | | | 5,902 | 65 | | |
| Labour costs | 2,724 | 30 | | | 2,724 | 30 | | | 2,724 | 30 | | |
| Fixed costs | 1,544 | 17 | | | 1,544 | 17 | | | 1,544 | 17 | | |
| Variable costs | 726 | 8 | | | 726 | 8 | | | 726 | 8 | | |
| Net profit | 908 | 10 | | | 9e8 | 10 | | | 908 | 10 | | |

By comparing the budget figures with the actual figures, the trend can be assessed, unusual variances can be investigated and an amended, more realistic budget can be prepared for the following periods. In the first year of a new business, the budget figures for the accounting periods will need to be constantly reviewed and revised if necessary. These amended figures will be the basis for planning the following year's budgets.

*Example 1:*
The following are the actual figures extracted from the books of the Atlanta Hotel for year 19 . . :

| | £ |
|---|---|
| Sales | 44,000 |
| Cost of sales | 16,280 |
| Labour costs | 14,080 |
| Fixed costs (rent, rates, insurance, depreciation) | 6,600 |
| Variable costs | 3,960 |
| Net profit | 3,080 |

191

For the coming year the management estimate a 10% increase in sales; a 65% gross profit margin is the target. By redistribution of labour, it is estimated that there will be a 2% reduction in labour costs. Fixed costs will increase by 1%. It is aimed to reduce variable costs by 2%. Prepare an estimated profit budget for sales for each quarter of the forthcoming year. Sales are estimated to be equal in the first and second half of the year, with quarters January to March and April to June in a 2:3 ratio, and quarters July to September and October to December are in a 5:3 ratio.

*Solution:*

Sales + 10% = £44,000 + £4,400 = £48,400
*Gross profit required:* 65%

$$\frac{65}{100} \times \frac{£48,400}{1} = £31,460$$

∴ *Cost of sales* = 35%

$$\frac{35}{100} \times \frac{£48,400}{1} = £16,940$$

Labour cost previous year = 32% of sales $\left( \dfrac{£14,080}{44,000} \times \dfrac{100}{1} \right)$

∴ *Labour cost this year if a 2% reduction is aimed for:* = 30%

$$\frac{30}{100} \times \frac{£48,400}{1} = £14,520$$

Fixed costs previous year = 15% of sales
∴ *Fixed costs this year if 1% increase is expected:*

$$\frac{16}{100} \times \frac{£48,400}{1} = £7,744$$

Variable costs previous year = 9% of sales
∴ *Variable costs this year if 2% reduction is aimed for:*

$$\frac{7}{100} \times \frac{£48,400}{1} = £3,388$$

Sales per half year

$$\frac{£48,400}{2} = £24,200$$

Sales 1st quarter

$$\frac{£24,200 \times 2}{5} = £9,680$$

Sales 2nd quarter

$$\frac{£24,200 \times 3}{5} = £14,520$$

Sales 3rd quarter

$$\frac{£24,200 \times 5}{8} = £15,125$$

Sales 4th quarter

$$\frac{£24,200 \times 3}{8} = £9,075$$

Fig. 13.3 Estimated profit budget (quarterly)

| | Jan.–Mar. | | Apr.–June | | July–Aug. | | Sept.–Dec. | | Total | |
|---|---|---|---|---|---|---|---|---|---|---|
| | £ | % | £ | % | £ | % | £ | % | £ | % |
| Sales | 9,680 | 100 | 14,520 | 100 | 15,125 | 100 | 9,075 | 100 | 48,400 | 100 |
| Cost of sales | 3,388 | 35 | 5,082 | 35 | 5,294 | 35 | 3,176 | 35 | 16,940 | 35 |
| Gross profit | 6,292 | 65 | 9,438 | 65 | 9,831 | 65 | 5,899 | 65 | 31,460 | 65 |
| Labour costs | 2,904 | 30 | 4,356 | 30 | 4,538 | 30 | 2,722 | 30 | 14,520 | 30 |
| Fixed costs | 1,936 | 20 | 1,936 | 13 | 1,936 | 13 | 1,936 | 21 | 7,744 | 16 |
| Variable costs | 678 | 7 | 1,016 | 7 | 1,059 | 7 | 635 | 7 | 3,388 | 7 |
| Net profit | 774 | 8 | 2,130 | 15 | 2,298 | 15 | 606 | 7 | 5,808 | 12 |

# Capital budgets

Capital budgets are concerned with changes in the assets and liabilities of the business. It is necessary to have co-ordinated plans for any expenditure on capital projects such as the purchase of new fixed assets. Since the implementation of such plans will depend on the finance available, assessment and classification into an order of priority will be applied to each project and consideration of the following factors is necessary when formulating plans:

(a) The purpose of the expenditure
(b) The effect the cost of the project will have on finance
(c) Estimated cost of the project
(d) What change there will be in the assets and liabilities of the business
(e) Whether the project is a necessity or optional.

When the budget for capital expenditure is set, each project within the budget will be controlled within the budget framework.

# Cash budgets

The object of the cash budget is to forecast and determine the forward cash position in order to plan the best use of the cash that will be available during the budget period. When expenditure on capital projects for expansion or large-scale maintenance is being planned, the timing of such plans is important from the point of view of the finance available. Consideration must be given as to what the cash position will be, whether overdrafts or additional finance will be necessary at high rates of interest, or whether surplus cash should be placed on deposit earning interest, instead of leaving it in the current account.

It must be remembered when preparing the cash budget that it is concerned only with estimating the cash inflow and cash outflow for each accounting period within the budget, and not with profitability or whether the amounts relate to that particular month. The effect on the bank balance for the month is our only concern in this instance.

## *Preparation of cash budgets*

1. Cash budgets are usually prepared for each accounting period.
2. The actual closing balance of the previous year is applied as the opening balance for the budget for the coming year.
3. Estimated net receipts from all sources are added to the opening balance and estimated net expenditure is deducted and the balance is carried forward to each accounting period.
4. Wages and salaries are normally paid in the month to which they refer.
5. Suppliers are usually paid on a basis of one month's credit, i.e. goods supplied in March would normally be paid for at the end of April.
6. Fixed expenses such as rates, rent, insurance are entered in the month on which payment falls due.
7. Sundry expenses are entered in the month in which they are paid.
8. Any capital expenditure planned is entered in the month when payment falls due.

*Example 2:*
  The following information is extracted from the operating and capital budgets of the Mayfair Hotel, and a cash budget for April, May and June accounting periods is prepared.

| Estimated receipts | Room sales | Food sales | Liquor sales | Other sales | Total |
|---|---|---|---|---|---|
| | £ | £ | £ | £ | £ |
| March | 1,200 | 960 | 192 | 48 | 2,400 |
| April | 2,000 | 1,600 | 320 | 80 | 4,000 |
| May | 2,800 | 2,240 | 448 | 112 | 5,600 |
| June | 3,200 | 2,560 | 512 | 128 | 6,400 |
| Totals | £9,200 | £7,360 | £1,472 | £368 | £18,400 |

| Estimated expenditure | Food purchases | Liquor purchases | Labour costs | Overheads | Total |
|---|---|---|---|---|---|
| | £ | £ | £ | £ | £ |
| March | 365 | 87 | 600 | 480 | 1,532 |
| April | 608 | 144 | 1,200 | 880 | 2,832 |
| May | 850 | 202 | 1,680 | 1,008 | 3,740 |
| June | 972 | 230 | 1,920 | 1,152 | 4,274 |
| Totals | £2,795 | £663 | £5,400 | £3,520 | £12,378 |

Fig. 13.4

*Notes:*
1. Opening Bank Balance 1 April, £5,750.
2. All receipts are assumed to be cash.
3. Payments for purchases and overheads are due in the month following.
4. Labour costs are paid in the same month to which they refer.
5. Interest due on investment £200 is anticipated in June.
6. Taxation of £750 is due to be paid in June.
7. A capital project for restaurant fixtures and fittings is planned for March; payment will be due: £1,500 in April, £1,500 in May.

|  |  | April | May | June |
|---|---|---:|---:|---:|
|  |  | £ | £ | £ |
| Opening balance b/f | | 5,750 | 6,118 | 6,906 |
| *Receipts:* | Room sales | 2,000 | 2,800 | 3,200 |
| | Food sales | 1,600 | 2,240 | 2,560 |
| | Liquor sales | 320 | 448 | 512 |
| | *Other sales* | 80 | 112 | 128 |
| | Interest | — | — | 200 |
| | **Total** | 9,750 | 11,718 | 13,506 |
| *Expenditure:* | Food purchases | 365 | 608 | 850 |
| | Liquor sales | 87 | 144 | 202 |
| | Labour costs | 1,200 | 1,680 | 1,920 |
| | Overhead cost | 480 | 880 | 1,008 |
| | Other expenditure | 1,500 | 1,500 | 750 |
| | **Total** | 3,632 | 4,812 | 4,730 |
| *Balance c/f* | | 6,118 | 6,906 | 8,776 |

Fig. 13.5   Estimated cash budget, April, May, June 19..

# Cash flow statements

Cash flow statements follow the same layout as a cash budget and are basically summarised statements showing the inflow and outflow of cash over a period of time. They are used as a control against the cash budget by periodical revisions, taking into consideration current cash balances and the most up-to-date forecasts of receipts and expenditure.

*Example 3:*

From the information provided in Fig. 13.5 the following cash flow statement can be prepared.

*Cash flow statement*

April to June 19 . .

|  | £ |
|---|---:|
| Total receipts | 16,200 |
| Total expenditure | 13,174 |
| Surplus at 30 June | 3,026 |
| *Add* Balance at 1 April | 5,750 |
| Forecast bank balance—30 June 19 . . | £8,776 |

If a cash budget has not been prepared, a cash flow statement can be prepared as follows:

1. Commence with the opening cash balance.
2. *Add* estimated net profit for the period, as it is assumed that the cash balance will increase by the estimated Net Profit after certain adjustments have been made. These adjustments are detailed below.
3. *Add* any interest expected from investments, as this is a cash receipt not taken into consideration in the profits budget.
4. *Add* any depreciation, as this is an expense deducted from net profit but not paid out in cash, therefore net profit figure would be increased by that amount.
5. *Add* any increase in creditors for the period and *deduct* any decrease in creditors. Creditors at the beginning of the period are added because they will be paid during the period under review, and creditors at the end are deducted because they will be paid in the next period:

*Example 4:*

Creditors at 1 April £932, Creditors at 30 June £2,354, means an increase in creditors of £1,422 which are added to the estimated cash balance, as they have been deducted from the net profit in the trading period but will not be paid during that period.

6. *Deduct* any capital expenditure or taxation as this is not taken into consideration in calculation of the net profit, but the payments will reduce the cash balance.

*Example 5:*

The estimated sales for Mayfair Hotel for the three months April–June are £16,200, Cost of sales £3,006, Labour cost £4,800, Overheads cost £3,040.

Sundry creditors 1 April £932
Sundry creditors 30 June £2,354
Depreciation on equipment £600
Capital expenditure on equipment £3,000
Income Tax payable in June £750
Opening cash balance 1 April £5,750

*Estimated profit statement*
April to June 19 . .

|  | £ | £ |
|---|---|---|
| Sales |  | 16,200 |
| *Less* cost of sales |  | 3,006 |
| Gross profit |  | 13,194 |
| Labour costs | 4,800 |  |
| Overhead costs | 3,040 |  |
| Depreciation | 600 |  |
|  |  | 8,440 |
|  |  | £4,754 |

*Cash flow statement*

April to June 19 . .

| | £ | £ |
|---|---|---|
| Estimated net profit | | 4,754 |
| *Add* Depreciation | 600 | |
| Increase in creditors | 1,422 | |
| | | 2,022 |
| | | 6,776 |
| *Less* Income Tax | 750 | |
| Capital expenditure | 3,000 | |
| | | 3,750 |
| Excess income over expenditure | | 3,026 |
| *Add* Opening balance at 1 April | | 5,750 |
| Forecast Bank Balance at 30 June | | £8,776 |

# Operating statements

Control can be exercised over all activities of the establishment by the use of a summary operating statement. This statement covers a specific period of time and sets out the budgeted income, expenditure and profit of each department, and the actual income, expenditure and profit. Continual comparison of budget against actual figures highlights the efficiency and progress of each department, and any variances can be investigated and corrective action taken where necessary.

## Preparation of an operating statement

1. These statements are usually prepared on a quarterly basis.
2. From the departmental operating statement for each activity, e.g. rooms, food, liquor, the following figures and percentages are extracted:
   (a) Net sales
   (b) Gross profit
   (c) Wages and staff costs
   (d) Net margin profit
   (e) The department's operating profit.
3. These budgeted and actual figures are entered on to the master summary operating statement and the total hotel operating profit can be ascertained.
4. Comparison of budget and actual figures will act as a control measure over all operations.

*Example 6:*

| 2nd Quarter | | | | | Year to date | | | |
| Budget | | Actual | | | Actual | | Budget | |
| £ | % | £ | % | | £ | % | £ | % |
|---|---|---|---|---|---|---|---|---|
| 6,400 | 100 | 6,200 | 100 | Net sales | 8,750 | 100 | 8,980 | 100 |
| 2,430 | 38 | 2,480 | 40 | *Less* Cost of sales | 3,500 | 40 | 3,412 | 38 |
| 3,970 | 62 | 3,720 | 60 | Gross profit | 5,250 | 60 | 5,568 | 62 |
| 1,920 | 30 | 1,736 | 28 | *Less* Labour costs | 2,625 | 30 | 2,694 | 30 |
| 2,050 | 32 | 1,984 | 32 | Net margin | 2,625 | 30 | 2,874 | 32 |
| 1,088 | 17 | 1,240 | 20 | *Less* Allocated expenses | 1,575 | 18 | 1,526 | 17 |
| 962 | 15 | 744 | 12 | Operating profit | 1,050 | 12 | 1,348 | 15 |

Fig. 13.6   Food Department operating statement

*Analysis:*
1. The actual sales are £200 less than budgeted sales for the quarter, and £230 less than the budget target for the year to date. The reason for this should be ascertained, as this is a 3% drop in sales and an unsatisfactory trend if it continues.
2. The food cost percentage has risen from 38% to 40%. Investigation into the kitchen operation is necessary to find the cause, e.g. wastage, bad portion control, pilfering, bad buying, etc.
3. The labour cost percentage dropped in the second quarter. Insufficient skilled staff could be one of the causes of the drop in sales.
4. The overhead expenses were 2% higher than the budgeted figure for the second quarter; this could be due to inclement weather causing an increase in heat, fuel and light, or it could be due to wastage by staff. The reason for the increase should be pinpointed, as the year to date figure is still 1% above the budget.
5. The 12% operating profit of the department is still 3% below the budget target of 15%; therefore the head of department must take appropriate action to see that this trend does not continue.

These figures are now transferred to the master operating statement for the hotel (Fig. 13.7).

| 2nd Quarter | | | | | To date | | | |
| Budget | | Actual | | Operating Departments | Actual | | Budget | |
| £ | % | £ | % | | £ | % | £ | % |
|---|---|---|---|---|---|---|---|---|
| | | | | Sales: | | | | |
| 8,000 | 51 | 7,945 | 52 | Rooms | 11,690 | 54 | 11,250 | 51 |
| 6,400 | 40 | 5,810 | 38 | Food | 8,230 | 38 | 8,980 | 40 |
| 1,280 | 9 | 1,525 | 10 | Liquor | 1,730 | 8 | 1,800 | 9 |
| 15,680 | 100 | 15,280 | 100 | Total net sales | 21,650 | 100 | 22,030 | 100 |
| | | | | Gross profit: | | | | |
| 8,000 | 100 | 7,945 | 100 | Rooms | 11,690 | 100 | 11,250 | 100 |
| 3,970 | 62 | 3,486 | 60 | Food | 5,250 | 60 | 5,568 | 62 |
| 704 | 55 | 793 | 52 | Liquor | 700 | 52 | 990 | 55 |
| 12,674 | 81 | 12,224 | 80 | Total gross profit | 17,640 | 81 | 17,808 | 81 |
| | | | | Labour costs: | | | | |
| 2,244 | 28 | 2,385 | 30 | Rooms | 3,510 | 30 | 3,150 | 28 |
| 1,920 | 30 | 1,740 | 30 | Food | 2,625 | 30 | 2,694 | 30 |
| 128 | 10 | 185 | 12 | Liquor | 208 | 12 | 180 | 10 |
| 4,292 | 27 | 4,310 | 28 | Total labour costs | 6,343 | 29 | 5,924 | 27 |
| | | | | Net margin: | | | | |
| 5,756 | 72 | 5,560 | 70 | Rooms | 8,180 | 70 | 8,100 | 72 |
| 2,050 | 32 | 1,746 | 30 | Food | 2,625 | 30 | 2,874 | 32 |
| 576 | 45 | 608 | 40 | Liquor | 492 | 40 | 810 | 45 |
| 8,382 | 54 | 7,914 | 52 | Total net margin | 11,297 | 52 | 11,784 | 54 |
| | | | | Department operating profit | | | | |
| 4,956 | 62 | 4,865 | 60 | Rooms | 7,010 | 60 | 6,975 | 62 |
| 962 | 15 | 744 | 12 | Food | 1,050 | 12 | 1,348 | 15 |
| 512 | 40 | 532 | 35 | Liquor | 406 | 35 | 770 | 40 |
| £6,430 | 41 | £6,141 | 40 | Total operating profit | £8,466 | 39 | £9,093 | 41 |

Fig. 13.7   Summary operating statement

# Progress test questions

1. (a) The seating capacity of the Bluebird Restaurant is 150; at the noon service 108 meals are served. What is the rate of seat occupancy?

   (b) The same restaurant serves lunch and dinner, and the number of meals served on an average day is 400—what is the rate and ratio of seat occupancy?

   (c) At lunch when 108 meals are served the takings amount to £253·80. What is the average spending power per customer?

2. (a) From the following information, prepare a customer projection chart and analysis of average seat occupancy, number of customers and takings:

   Maximum seating capacity of restaurant—150 customers
   Average spending power per customer—£2·45

   |           | Number of customers |
   |-----------|---------------------|
   | Monday    | 84                  |
   | Tuesday   | 93                  |
   | Wednesday | 90                  |
   | Thursday  | 108                 |
   | Friday    | 132                 |
   | Saturday  | 150                 |

   (b) From the customer projection chart estimate the average yearly turnover, if management are working on a 65% gross profit margin. Labour costs are estimated at 25%, Fixed costs 18% and Variable costs 7% of sales. The year is divided into 13 accounting periods. Prepare an estimated profits budget for accounting periods 1, 2 and 3.

3. The following figures are extracted from the accounts of the Carillon Hotel for the year ending 31 December 19 . . :

   Sales £35,000, Cost of sales £21,700, Labour costs £9,800, Fixed costs £5,250, Variable costs £2,100.

   For the coming year management estimate a 5% increase in sales, and a 65% gross profit margin is the target. Labour costs are expected to increase by 2% and variable costs by 1%. Fixed costs are expected to remain constant. Prepare an estimated profit budget for the four quarters January–March, April–June, July–September and October–December.

4. The following data are extracted from the operating budgets of the Swan Hotel:

### Estimated receipts

|  | Room sales £ | Food sales £ | Liquor sales £ | Other sales £ |
|---|---|---|---|---|
| June | 4,000 | 2,950 | 720 | 80 |
| July | 4,400 | 3,200 | 800 | 130 |
| August | 4,600 | 3,400 | 910 | 160 |
| September | 4,500 | 3,150 | 830 | 180 |

### Estimated expenditure

|  | Food purchases £ | Liquor purchases £ | Labour cost £ | Overheads £ |
|---|---|---|---|---|
| June | 1,180 | 324 | 2,325 | 1,395 |
| July | 1,216 | 360 | 2,560 | 1,535 |
| August | 1,360 | 410 | 2,720 | 1,632 |
| September | 1,197 | 374 | 2,600 | 1,560 |

Notes:
1. The opening cash balance is £6,200.
2. Assume all receipts are cash.
3. Payments for overheads and purchases are due in the month following.
4. Labour costs are paid in the month to which they refer.
5. An Income Tax demand of £600 is due to be paid in September.
6. Capital expenditure on kitchen equipment valued at £2,000 will be due for payment £1,250 in July, £750 in September.
7. Interest £150 due on investments is expected in June.

(a) Prepare an estimated cash budget for July, August and September.
(b) From the information in the cash budget prepare a cash flow statement.

5. From the following information prepare an estimated profit statement and cash flow statement for the year ended 31 March 19 . . for the Flamingo Restaurant:

Sales for the financial year are estimated at £42,000. Food cost is estimated at 38% of sales, Labour cost 28% of sales, Rent payable will be £2,450 per annum, Rates are £950 per annum, Insurance premiums are £450 per annum.

Depreciation at 10% must be provided on Equipment £10,000 (cost).

Variable expenses are estimated at 12% of sales.

Sundry creditors at 31 March this year amounted to £4,500 and it is estimated that sundry creditors next year will be £2,250.

Equipment to be purchased during the financial year will cost £2,000.
The Income Tax liability, payable on 1 January, amounts to £1,825.
The opening balance at the bank on 1 April is £7,250.

6. Complete the following food department operating statement for the third quarter and comment on your findings.

| 3rd Quarter Budget £ | % | Actual £ | % | | Year to date Budget £ | % | Actual £ | % |
|---|---|---|---|---|---|---|---|---|
| 4,000 | | 3,000 | | Net sales | 10,500 | | 10,000 | |
| | 35 | 1,200 | — | Cost of sales | | 35 | 3,750 | — |
| | | | | Gross profit | | | | |
| | 30 | 920 | — | Direct labour | | 30 | 3,200 | — |
| | | | | Net margin | | | | |
| | 20 | 800 | | Overheads all'n | | 20 | 2,200 | — |
| | | | | Operating profit | | | | |

7. (a) What is the purpose of the master summary operating statement?
   (b) Itemise the detail necessary for the preparation of the summary operating statement and the source of the information.

# CHAPTER 14

# Operating Budgets

## The sales budget

This budget is the most important and the most difficult to prepare, as it is the key to the profits budget and will vitally affect the preparation of all other operating budgets.

### Preparation of the budget

When preparing the sales budget it is necessary to analyse and assess the following data and information:

1. The sales figures for previous years.
2. The sales mix percentages and their current trends.
3. The limiting factors which could prevent an increase in sales.
4. The availability of labour in relation to any budgeted increase in sales.
5. The availability of accommodation and seating capacity of the establishment in relation to any proposed increase in demand.
6. Other information regarding conditions of local employment and prosperity, and the economic situation of the country in general. Any future government policies which could affect any future sales.
7. The sales policy of the hotel with regard to special function business, reduced rates in the 'off-season', coach parties, etc.

### Sales analysis

The first step in the preparation of the sales budget is a study of the detailed analysis of past sales.

*Example 1:*

*Stanmore Hotel*

Sales analysis for past four years

| Department | 1973 | Increase/ Decrease last year | 1974 | Increase/ Decrease last year | 1975 | Increase/ Decrease last year | 1976 | Increase/ Decrease last year |
|---|---|---|---|---|---|---|---|---|
| | £ | % | £ | % | £ | % | £ | % |
| Rooms | 32,000 | +1 | 32,600 | +2 | 34,272 | +5 | 36,672 | +7 |
| Restaurants | 25,600 | +2 | 26,880 | +5 | 28,224 | +5 | 29,636 | +5 |
| Bars | 5,120 | +2 | 5,428 | +6 | 5,808 | +7 | 6,102 | +5 |
| Other sales | 1,280 | +3 | 1,320 | +3 | 1,400 | +6 | 1,470 | +5 |
| Total sales | £64,000 | +2 | £66,228 | +3·4 | £69,704 | +5 | £73,880 | +6 |

*Analysis:*

1. *Room sales.* There has been a steady percentage increase on each previous year.
2. *Food sales.* There has been a steady 5% increase each year. This is attributable to increase in prices rather than increase in volume of sales.
3. *Bar sales.* A drop of 2% in the rate of increase compared with the previous year indicates a need for investigation and analysis of bar sales so that there is no further downward trend in the rate of growth.
4. *Other sales.* A drop of 1% in the rate of growth compared with the previous year calls for an analysis of the sales so that the trend does not continue.

## Determination of sales targets

1. *Room sales.* A maximum occupancy has yet to be reached. It is felt that by a well directed advertising campaign, offering more competitive prices for the winter tariff, and more attractive terms for conferences and special functions during the off season, a target of a 10% increase on turnover could be set for the forthcoming year.
2. *Restaurant sales.* Dining room space is limited, but a capital project to redesign and enlarge the area is planned and expected to be completed in time for the on season. Prices will also need to be revised to counteract increasing food prices. It is decided to aim for a 7% increase on the previous year.
3. *Bar sales.* Investigation has shown that lack of efficient staff could be the reason for the poor sales; this must be rectified. Bar prices will need revision to counteract increase in prices. It is decided to aim for a 4% increase in sales.
4. *Other sales.* The rate of increase in this activity is falling off and it is felt that a further increase will prove difficult.

In consideration of these factors the budgeted figures for 1977 would be:

*Sales budget 1977*

| | | |
|---|---|---|
| Room sales 1976 + 10% = £36,672 + £3,668 | = | £40,340 |
| Restaurant sales 1976 + 7% = £29,636 + £2,074 = | | £31,710 |
| Bar sales + 4% = £6,102 + £244 | = | £6,346 |
| Other sales 1976 + 5% = £1,470 + £74 | = | £1,544 |
| | Total sales | £79,940 |

The budgeted sales are then broken down into the accounting periods (13).

*Monthly sales budget*

|  | £ | | | £ |
|---|---|---|---|---|
| Rooms | $\frac{40,340}{13}$ = 3,103 | say | 3,100 |
| Restaurant | $\frac{31,710}{13}$ = 2,440 | | 2,440 |
| Bars | $\frac{6,346}{13}$ = 488 | say | 490 |
| Other sales | $\frac{1,544}{13}$ = 119 | say | 120 |
| | | | | £6,150 |

Control would be exercised over sales by the preparation of monthly comparative reports.

*Monthly comparative report*
4 weeks ending 30 May 19. .

| Department | Budget £ | % | Actual £ | % | Variance ± £ | % |
|---|---|---|---|---|---|---|
| Rooms | 3,100 | 50 | 3,000 | 48 | − 100 | − 3 |
| Restaurant | 2,440 | 40 | 2,438 | 39 | − 2 | − 0·1 |
| Bars | 490 | 8 | 625 | 10 | + 135 | + 28 |
| Other sales | 120 | 2 | 187 | 3 | + 67 | + 56 |
| Total | £6,150 | 100 | 6,250 | 100 | + 100 | + 1·6 |

*Analysis:*

1. *Room sales.* The actual results are 3% short of target. Actual sales and advance bookings should be analysed to see if this is also indicative of the future trend. Possible causes for the downward trend could be:

   (a) Inefficient selling by the reception department;
   (b) Insufficient or badly directed advertising;
   (c) Competitors' prices;
   (d) Trade disputes or economic crisis in the country causing a drop in consumer spending;
   (e) The number of rooms available for letting, e.g. some rooms could be in the process of redecorating or maintenance repairs.

Whatever the cause, it should be noted and appropriate action taken if necessary.

2. *Restaurant sales.* The 0·1% deviation from target could be due to a seasonal fluctuation but a watchful eye should be kept to ensure the deviation does not increase.
3. *Bar sales.* An increase of 28% over target indicates that the staffing problems that existed have been remedied and these sales are on an upward trend.
4. *Other sales.* An increase of 56% over target also indicates an upward trend.

# Seasonal establishments

Sales may vary during the year if the establishment is seasonal. When preparing the budget a study of past years' figures and trends will indicate the average percentage of the total yearly sales attributable to each month or quarter and the estimated budget can be prepared accordingly.

*Example 2:*

Estimated yearly sales budget 1977

| | £ | % of total sales (to nearest whole number) |
|---|---|---|
| Room sales | 40,340 | 50 |
| Restaurant sales | 31,710 | 40 |
| Bar sales | 6,346 | 8 |
| Other sales | 1,544 | 2 |
| Total sales | £79,940 | 100 |

Estimated quarterly sales budget

| Department | Jan. to Mar. | % of sales | April to June | % of sales | July to Sept. | % of sales | Oct. to Dec. | % of sales | Total £ |
|---|---|---|---|---|---|---|---|---|---|
| Room sales | 7,994 | 50 | 11,991 | 50 | 12,391 | 50 | 7,594 | 50 | 40,340 |
| Restaurant sales | 6,395 | 40 | 9,593 | 40 | 9,913 | 40 | 6,075 | 40 | 31,710 |
| Bar sales | 1,279 | 8 | 1,918 | 8 | 1,982 | 8 | 1,215 | 8 | 6,346 |
| Other sales | 320 | 2 | 480 | 2 | 496 | 2 | 304 | 2 | 1,544 |
| Total | 15,988 | 100 | 23,982 | 100 | 24,782 | 100 | 15,188 | 100 | 79,940 |
| % of total sales | 20% | | 30% | | 31% | | 19% | | 100% |

*Note:*
If the sales mix, e.g. 50% room sales, 40% restaurant sales, 8% bar sales, other sales 2%, vary with the seasonal fluctuation, past figures will indicate the variance and the budgeted figures will be amended accordingly.

# Labour cost budget

The labour cost percentage of sales for providing personal services in hotels and restaurants will vary with:

(a)  The standard of service and cuisine provided by the establishment.
(b)  Staff requirements in relation to rate of occupancy and seating capacity.
(c)  If the establishment is seasonal the labour cost percentage will vary with the fluctuation in turnover during the 'on' and 'off' season, for example:

| | |
|---|---|
| April | 42% |
| May | 38% |
| June | 35% |
| July | 30% |
| August | 24% |
| September | 28% |

(d)  The productivity and efficiency of staff will have an effect on the labour cost percentage. The amount of effective work done by the staff is usually within the control of the supervisors, and trained heads of department ensure that the work is planned and that the staff work efficiently and at a reasonable rate. In the hotel and catering industry, as elsewhere, the training of staff results in a higher standard of service, improved productivity and efficiency.

## *Preparation of the budget*

It must be remembered that the cost of an employee to an establishment is not limited to his gross pay; the employer's National Insurance contribution, holiday pay, pension fund contributions, staff meals, liquor, accommodation and uniforms where applicable are additional costs.

As with other budgets all known facts are taken into account. The actual wages for the previous year are used as a basis and calculated as a percentage of the sales figure:

*Example 3:*

$$\frac{\text{Wages}}{\text{Sales}} = \frac{£39,300}{£131,040} \times \frac{100}{1} = 30\%$$

To prepare a realistic labour cost budget it is also necessary to take into consideration the following factors:

1.  Details of number and grades of staff employed by each department.
2.  The current rates of pay for each grade of staff.
3.  The cost of any authorised overtime and casual labour employed.

4. Any anticipated national pay awards in the forthcoming year.
5. Any expected statutory National Insurance contribution increases in the forthcoming budget period.
6. Any staff reorganisation proposed.
7. Whether any proposed increase in budgeted sales will be within the scope of existing staff or necessitate employing more staff.

When all these factors have been taken into consideration a budget can be prepared.

*Example 4:*
At the end of the year the following labour cost statement was prepared by the wages department for the information of the management of the Hadley Hotel Ltd.

*Labour cost statement*

for year ending 31 December 19 . .

| Department | £ | % |
|------------|------|-----|
| Reception | 5,895 | 15 |
| Porterage | 3,144 | 8 |
| Housekeeping | 11,790 | 30 |
| Bars | 2,751 | 7 |
| Restaurant | 7,074 | 18 |
| Kitchen | 8,646 | 22 |
| Totals | £39,300 | 100% |

(*Note:* These totals include the indirect labour which is apportioned in ratio between all departments.)

The turnover for that year was £131,040 and the total labour cost thus represents 30% of sales. The sales budget for the forthcoming year has been prepared on the basis of a 5% increase on turnover, i.e. £131,040 + 5% = £137,592 (say £137,600). After due consideration of all known factors which include an expected national pay award and an increase in the standard rate of National Insurance contributions, the labour costs for the coming year are expected to rise by at least 2% of sales. The total budgeted labour costs will therefore amount to 32% of £137,600 equalling £44,032. On this basis the budgeted labour cost for each department for the forthcoming year would be as follows:

| Last year actual | | Department | This year budget | | Actual | | Deviation | |
|---|---|---|---|---|---|---|---|---|
| £ | % | | £ | % | £ | % | + | − |
| 5,895 | 15 | Reception | 6,605 | 15 | | | | |
| 3,144 | 8 | Porterage | 3,523 | 8 | | | | |
| 11,790 | 30 | Housekeeping | 13,210 | 30 | | | | |
| 2,751 | 7 | Bars | 3,082 | 7 | | | | |
| 7,074 | 18 | Restaurant | 7,925 | 18 | | | | |
| 8,646 | 22 | Kitchen | 9,687 | 22 | | | | |
| 39,300 | 100 | Totals | 44,032 | 100 | | | | |

Total sales £

Total labour cost
as a % of sales:                    %

The budgeted labour cost for each department is divided into accounting periods (say 13), e.g.:

Housekeeping   $\frac{£13,210}{13} = £1,016$ per 4-week period

To provide an effective method of control a weekly labour cost statement is prepared for each department. The total wages paid will be calculated and the total for the four-week period will be compared to the budget target. Heads of department will have the responsibility of keeping their labour costs within the target and a watchful eye is kept on the amount of overtime worked and casual labour employed so that the budget figure is not exceeded.

If the establishment is seasonal, the labour costs are budgeted in ratio to the fluctuations during the season.

# Overheads cost budget

This budget is prepared in the same manner as other budgets. The figures for the previous year are used as a basis and all known factors are taken into consideration. When the departmental budgets are prepared direct expenses are allocated to the appropriate department and indirect expenses are allocated either in proportion to sales or apportioned on a basis of floor area. In small establishments one overheads budget would cover all overheads; however, in large organisations separate budgets would be prepared for various types of expenditure such as advertising, administration and office costs, and maintenance. A fixed amount is usually budgeted for this kind of expense and control is exercised by comparison of budget with actual expenditure to ensure the budgeted amount is not exceeded.

*Example 5:*

### Advertising Budget
for year 19.. £3,200

| 3rd quarter | | | | | Year to date | | | |
|---|---|---|---|---|---|---|---|---|
| Budget | | Actual | | | Actual | | Budget | |
| £ | % | £ | % | | £ | % | £ | % |
| 224 | 28 | 238 | 28 | Labour cost | 700 | 28 | 672 | 28 |
| 32 | 4 | 25 | 3 | Press advertising | 125 | 5 | 96 | 4 |
| 288 | 36 | 272 | 32 | Brochures and circulars | 850 | 34 | 864 | 36 |
| 96 | 12 | 85 | 10 | Postage and envelopes | 250 | 10 | 288 | 12 |
| 16 | 2 | 17 | 2 | Posters | 50 | 2 | 48 | 2 |
| 40 | 5 | 60 | 7 | Travelling expenses | 175 | 7 | 120 | 5 |
| 40 | 5 | 68 | 8 | Entertaining expenses | 150 | 6 | 120 | 5 |
| 64 | 8 | 85 | 10 | Fees and services | 200 | 8 | 192 | 8 |
| 800 | 100 | 850 | 100 | | 2,500 | 100 | 2,400 | 100 |

*Analysis:*
The actual expenses are exceeding the budgeted expenditure in the third quarter by £100. In the last quarter this will have to be offset with particular attention to the curtailment of travelling and entertaining expenses.

# Housekeeping budget

This budget will be prepared in relation to the room sales and rate of occupancy and will have to consider the labour cost of all housekeeping staff, cost of linen, laundry and replacements, cleaning materials and floral decorations and other sundry expenses related to housekeeping.

# Maintenance budget

Small establishments usually employ staff to provide maintenance service only and any major repairs are undertaken by specialist contractors. These expenses are usually taken into consideration in the overheads budgets. Large organisations usually prepare a separate maintenance budget. This will be done after consideration of the following factors.

1. Maintenance labour costs
2. Cost of maintenance materials and supplies
3. Other costs, including depreciation of equipment
4. Planned maintenance usually done by outside contractors such as redecorations, painting, etc.

A well planned maintenance budget will not only exercise control over the expenditure on maintenance and repairs but will also show the plan of routine maintenance work that has to be carried out over the budget period.

# Progress test questions

1. Detail the factors that will need to be taken into consideration when preparing the sales budgets.

2. (a) Complete the following sales analysis table and comment on your findings.

*Sales Analysis*

| 1974 | Increase on previous year | 1975 | Increase on previous year | Department | 1976 | Increase on previous year |
|---|---|---|---|---|---|---|
| £ | % | £ | % | | £ | % |
| 32,960 | 3 | 34,608 | | Rooms | 37,030 | |
| 24,206 | 2 | 24,690 | | Restaurants | 25,184 | |
| 6,300 | 5 | 6,426 | | Bars | 6,490 | |
| 2,040 | 2 | 2,080 | | Other sales | 2,122 | |
| | | | | Totals | | |

(b) From the completed sales analysis table prepare a sales budget for the forthcoming year after taking the following into consideration:

  (i) Management decide to set a target of a 10% increase on room sales;

  (ii) An extension is planned for the restaurant, and it is estimated a 4% increase in sales should be the result;

  (iii) A 3% increase is to be aimed for in bar sales;

  (iv) It is felt that no improvement can be made on 'other sales'.

3. Explain briefly how the cost of an employee differs from the wages paid to the employee.

4. Detail the factors that will need to be considered when preparing a labour cost budget.

5. (a) From the following figures supplied by the Wages Department prepare a labour cost statement for the year ending 31 December, 19 . .

| Department | Actual wages (incl. apportioned wages) |
|---|---|
| Front office reception | £7,812 |
| Housekeeping/Porterage | £13,888 |
| Bars | £4,340 |
| Restaurant | £6,944 |
| Kitchen | £10,416 |

  (b) If the turnover was £155,000, calculate the labour cost as a percentage of sales.

  (c) The sales budget for the forthcoming year has been prepared and a 7% increase on sales is the target set. After consideration of all known facts the labour cost total percentage is expected to increase by 2%. From this information prepare a labour cost budget for the forthcoming year, presuming that the departmental percentages of the total labour cost will remain the same.

6. Detail the factors you would need to consider when preparing the following budgets:

  (a) An overheads budget
  (b) A housekeeping budget
  (c) A maintenance budget.

7. From the following information complete the room sales operating budget.

| Actual 1976 | | Account | Budget 1977 | |
|---|---|---|---|---|
| £ | % | | £ | % |
| 36,000 | 100 | Net room sales | | |
| 9,750 | 27 | Labour costs | | |
| | | *Expenses* | | |
| 360 | 1·0 | Uniforms | | |
| 900 | 2·5 | Laundry | | |
| 540 | 1·5 | Linen | | |
| 360 | 1·0 | Cleaning materials | | |
| 360 | 1·0 | Replacement | | |
| 720 | 2·0 | Allocated commission payable | | |
| 360 | 1·0 | Miscellaneous expenses | | |
| 3,600 | 10·0 | Total expenses | | |
| 22,650 | 63·0 | Department operating profit | | |

Notes:
1. Budgeted room sales are expected to show a 5% increase on the previous year.
2. The labour cost percentage is expected to increase to 30% of sales.
3. The laundry and linen cost percentages are both expected to increase by 0·5% on budgeted sales.
4. The other expenses percentages are expected to remain constant.

# CHAPTER 15

# Industrial Catering

## Canteens and subsidies

It is the policy of many large companies to provide catering facilities for their employees, as it has been realised that productivity and efficiency are related to the welfare and wellbeing of the workers. Therefore a great deal of money is spent in equipping kitchens and dining rooms to provide low cost meals, the companies usually subsidising any losses made by the provision of the services.

There are several methods by which organisations can provide these catering facilities:

1. A catering department can be set up within the company, the cost of equipment, labour, and other expenses being borne by the company. If different standards of catering are to be provided, e.g. a directors' dining room, waitress service for executives, self-service restaurants and tea trolley and snack bar services, it is usual to have a centralised kitchen providing all food. Each unit is costed separately and has to produce weekly or monthly trading results. The company sometimes allocates a fixed sum as a subsidy. Budgets are prepared for each operation and the catering manager has the responsibility of seeing that costs are contained within the budgets. By this means control is exercised over the level of the subsidies.

2. Another method is for the company to invite tenders from industrial caterers for the provision of catering services to the company. The facilities and equipment, and possibly labour and other costs, could be paid for by the company, and for a fee the caterers will provide a catering manager who will organise and run the operation. When tenders are submitted for the contract, specific details must be itemised of exactly what services are being provided by the caterer. As the object is the provision of meals at low cost, a weekly or monthly statement of all costs is usually submitted to the company so that the extent of the subsidy to cover any canteen losses is determined.

3. In some cases the company could provide floor space to an outside catering organisation at a nominal rent. The equipment, labour, overheads and other costs are borne by the caterer. The prices of the meals are fixed in conjunction with the company and any loss is met by the company in the form of a subsidy.

Whatever method of catering is chosen, the extent of the subsidy and whether it is a fixed amount to offset losses or given in the form of luncheon vouchers to the employees is a management policy decision, and this decision can only be reached after consideration of all known factors and information.

*Example 1:*
The management of a large company have decided to provide catering facilities for their 400 employees.

1. It is estimated that 70% of the employees will use the canteen 5 days a week, 50 weeks per annum.
2. A lunch menu with a limited choice of dishes will be offered at self-service counters, the food cost for an average meal not to exceed 40p.
3. Cost of gas, electricity, heat, cutlery, crockery, glassware replacements, cleaning materials, laundry and other sundry expenses including depreciation of equipment is estimated at £6,000 per annum.
4. A catering manageress is to be appointed at £2,500 per annum. The wages for kitchen and counter staff are estimated at £270 per week, 52 weeks per year.

The catering manageress has been asked to prepare a statement setting out details of costs, so that a pricing policy can be formulated, and the extent of the necessary subsidy considered.

*Solution:*
*Statement of costs and sales for canteen*
Estimated number of meals to be provided:

$$\frac{70}{100} \times 400 = 280 \text{ meals daily}$$

Estimated number of meals per annum:
280 × 5 days × 50 weeks = 70,000 meals

| | | | |
|---|---|---|---|
| Food cost: 70,000 × 40p | = | | £28,000 |
| Labour cost:   1 Catering manageress | = | £2,500 | |
|     Kitchen and counter staff | | | |
|     £270 × 52 weeks | = | £14,040 | |
| | | | £16,540 |
| Overheads cost: | | | £6,000 |
| Total sales required to cover costs | = | | £50,540 |

Average selling price per meal would need to be:

$$\frac{\text{Required sales}}{\text{No. of meals}} = \frac{£50,540}{70,000} = 77 \cdot 2\text{p} \,(78\text{p})$$

On consideration of the statement, the management have decided that the charge to the employee for a 3-course lunch would be 45p. The subsidy provided by the management is therefore

$$78 - 45p = 33p \text{ per meal}$$
$$= 70,000 \times 33p = £23,100 \text{ per annum}$$
$$\frac{£23,100}{£50,540} = 45 \cdot 7\% \text{ of sales}$$

*Example 2:*

The Echo Tool Company proposes providing canteen facilities for its employees.

1. It is estimated that 90% of the 900 employees will use the canteen, 5 days a week, 50 weeks per annum.
2. Floor space will be rented to an industrial catering organisation for a nominal sum of £5,000 per annum.
3. The management will expend capital to pay for the equipping of the kitchen and canteen and will also pay for insurance and replacements, but all other expenses will have to be met by the caterer.
4. Menus have been planned to provide lunch with a limited choice, the food cost for an average meal not to exceed 35p.
5. A catering manager will be paid a salary of £3,000 per annum and wages for the kitchen and counter staff will average £400 per week, 52 weeks per annum.
6. Electricity and gas are estimated at £2,000 per annum, and other expenses estimated at £1,125 per annum. (Depreciation costs will be borne by the management.)
7. The caterer, in view of the guaranteed turnover, is prepared to accept a net profit of £5,400 per annum (approximately 5% on turnover).
8. Any other income from the sale of teas and snacks will be additional profit for the caterer on the understanding that prices are kept to the minimum.

The catering manager is asked to prepare for the company a statement detailing estimated costs, profit and required average spending per employee necessary to meet all costs. From this information the management will make a policy decision as to what extent and what form any subsidy will take to enable the employees to take advantage of the catering facilities.

*Solution:*

*Canteen estimated cost and profit statement*

Estimated number of meals to be provided:

$$\frac{90}{100} \times 900 = 810 \text{ meals daily}$$

Estimated number of meals per annum:
810 × 5 days × 50 weeks = 202,500 meals

|  |  |  | £ | £ |
|---|---|---|---|---|
| Food cost: 202,500 × 35p | | = | | 70,875 |
| Labour cost: | 1 Catering manager | = | 3,000 | |
| | Kitchen and counter staff | | | |
| | £400 × 52 weeks | = | 20,800 | |
| | | | | 23,800 |
| Other costs: | Rent | = | 5,000 | |
| | Electricity, gas | = | 2,000 | |
| | Other expenses | = | 1,125 | |
| | | | | 8,125 |
| Total | | = | | £102,800 |

The caterer requires 5% on turnover as net profit
∴ £102,800 represents 95% (sales 100%)

$$\therefore \frac{£102,800}{95} \times \frac{100}{1} = £108,210 \text{ total sales}$$

This is the return the canteen requires to meet all costs and the caterer's profit.

Dividing this by the number of meals will give the average spending per meal required.

$$\frac{£108,210}{202,500} = 53.4p \, (54p)$$

After consideration of these factors the management decide to subsidise the canteen to the extent of providing luncheon vouchers valued at 35p to employees which can only be used for the purchase of a lunch. The annual estimated cost of the subsidy to the company is 202,500 × 35p = £70,875. Items will be priced individually and if the total cost of the meal exceeds 35p, the difference has to be met by the employee. In this manner it is felt that the employee has a choice of menu instead of a fixed meal at a fixed low cost, and the additional 19p per head necessary to meet total costs will be recovered by the overall food, soft drinks and other sales in the canteen.

It must be appreciated that the cost to the company is not only the subsidy to cover any trading loss, but also the cost of providing any equipment, use of premises and any other expenses that are paid for by the company.

Many companies in close proximity share catering facilities. This can be to their mutual benefit, for the greater the turnover, the more the fixed costs are distributed, thus reducing the cost of producing the meals, which in turn will reduce the subsidies required.

# Airline catering

The growth and development of air travel throughout the world has resulted in large catering organisations signing special contracts to meet the demands of the airlines for the provision of meals for their passengers.

Many airlines provide their own equipment, cutlery, china, glassware, etc., and many overseas airlines also provide their own specialised food from their own countries to be incorporated in the menus.

From the point of view of cost control, the standard of meal will be in ratio to the fare paid, and the caterer will contract to provide a certain standard of meal for a set price. In economy or tourist class great use is made of pre-portioned food which aids portion and cost control, as it reduces wastage, washing up and breakages. All meals are completely standardised with all portions identical and it is a simple matter to cost and fix a realistic selling price to the airlines.

# Ships catering

Ship-board catering is vastly different from shore catering. The ship has to be victualled (stocked) to cater for a fixed number of passengers for a certain number of meals which could mean possibly 1,200 passengers for breakfast, lunch, afternoon teas and dinner every day of a voyage. Catering on such a scale has to be planned and highly organised. Menus are usually prepared and costed by the catering department of head office, and the ship is re-victualled after every voyage according to the menu requirements for the next voyage.

As the fare per passenger includes the cost of food and accommodation, a percentage of the fares is allocated to food cost. Catering officers on board ship have the authority to purchase at advantageous prices fresh fruit and vegetables through the ship's agents at the ship's ports of call.

As with every large-scale catering operation, cost control must be exercised at all times. The food and beverage controllers have an allowance per day per passenger and these targets act as a form of budgetary control.

It must be remembered that large passenger liners can carry a ship's complement of between 300 and 600 officers and crew. Officers usually take the same meals as the passengers and the allowance per head would be the same. Other crew have their own separate galley and catering facilities and the cost of providing meals for the crew is also based on an allowance per head, obviously lower than that estimated for the passengers and officers. In the final analysis, the cost of providing meals for officers and crew is regarded as a labour cost, the same as in any other catering establishment.

Strict control is kept over issue of supplies from stores to galley (kitchen), and menu counts and other statistics have to be kept to provide information and data for head office.

Fig. 15.1    Shipboard catering—menu count

<table>
<tr><td colspan="5" style="text-align:center">Menu Count</td></tr>
<tr>
<td>VESSEL M.S. atlantis<br>DATE 14.7.19<br>NUMBER OF PASSENGERS 820</td>
<td colspan="4">VOYAGE NUMBER 670<br>MENU NUMBER 17<br>WEATHER Cool</td>
</tr>
</table>

| DINNER ITEMS (HOT) | NO OF PORTIONS | NO SERVED | AMOUNT ORDERED | USED |
|---|---|---|---|---|
| Sirloin strips | 10 to ½ strip | 457 | 50½ strips | 460 used |
| Racks of lamb | 2 orders per rack | 204 | 4 cases – 30 racks per case | 3¾ cases |
| Duck | 4 portions per duck | 78 | 25 | 20 |
| Trout | Individual | 64 | 70 | 64 |
| Cold Buffet | | 17 | | |

# School meal catering

It has been for many years a statutory duty of local education authorities to provide school meals for children up to and including secondary school age. The aim of this service is to provide a well-balanced meal of the required nutritional standard within strict cost limits.

A school meals organiser is responsible for advising each authority on the organisation and smooth running of the service. Purchasing of supplies and equipment is usually by contract, and laid down by the policy of the local authority.

Meals may be cooked and served on the school premises or in centralised kitchens and distributed to a group of schools.

School meals are costed per unit as in industry, and originally parents contributed nominally to the food cost, the government meeting the cost of labour and overheads. However, in view of the continual rise of prices, the cost of providing the service is under constant review and many changes are foreseen in the future.

# Hospital catering

Hospital catering is classified as welfare catering, the object being to assist the hospital staff to get the patient well as soon as possible. Catering officers are responsible for menu planning, purchasing, the organisation of work and control of staff.

The catering officer has a budget of a maximum amount of money that can be spent based on a fixed sum per head, and it requires a great deal of skill, judgement and experience to keep within the budget available. As with school meals catering, the cost of providing the service is constantly under review by the Government.

# Progress test questions

1. Explain briefly three different methods a company could use to provide catering facilities for use by their employees.

2. The Sullivan Electrical Company are considering providing catering facilities for their 625 employees. From the following information prepare a cost statement setting out details, and showing the estimated subsidy that will be needed to offset any canteen loss.

   (a) It is estimated that 80% of the employees will use the canteen.
   (b) Floor space will be rented to an industrial caterer for a nominal sum of £4,000 p.a.
   (c) The company will equip the kitchen and canteen.
   (d) A catering manager will be appointed at £3,500 p.a.
   (e) The caterer will be responsible to the company for an apportioned cost of £1,500 p.a. to cover gas, electricity, heating and water; other sundry expenses are estimated at £1,500 p.a.
   (f) Basic menus have been planned, the food cost for a simple 3-course lunch not to exceed 30p.
   (g) Wages cost for kitchen and counter staff is estimated at £250 per week for 52 weeks per year.
   (h) The caterer will accept an 8% net profit on turnover in view of guaranteed sales.
   (i) It is decided to sell the meals at a fixed cost of 35p.

3. The Acme Engineering Company Ltd operates a works canteen which caters for approximately 250 employees 5 days a week 50 weeks per annum who take a simple 3-course lunch at a fixed price of 40p, the food cost of which is 30p per meal. The company has equipped the kitchen and canteen and the following costs are incurred:

   | | |
   |---|---|
   | Depreciation on equipment | £2,500 p.a. |
   | Gas, electricity, water | £1,200 p.a. |
   | Sundry expenses | £600 p.a. |

*Labour costs* (52 weeks)

    1 Catering manageress @ £60 per week
    4 Kitchen staff @ £40 per week each
    3 Counter staff @ £25 per week each
    1 Cashier @ £25 per week

(a) Prepare a statement of costs and sales for the canteen, and show the estimated subsidy required to cover any loss.

(b) The ABC Furnishing Company on the same trading estate have approached the Acme Engineering Co. Ltd. and asked if they would consider offering the same catering services to their 125 employees; the ABC Furnishing Co. would be prepared to share equally any subsidy required to meet canteen losses. The facilities are more than adequate to cater for the additional meals to be prepared. Gas and electricity are estimated to cost an additional £300 p.a., sundry expenses an additional £200 p.a., while 1 extra. member of kitchen staff @ £40 p.w., 1 extra counter staff @ £25 p.w. and 1 extra cashier @ £25 p.w. would be required. Depreciation would not be affected. Prepare a statement of costs and sales showing details of the effect of catering for the additional 125 people, and show how the subsidy of the Acme Engineering Co. Ltd would be affected.

4. Describe briefly how catering for airlines and catering for ocean-going liners differ from usual catering methods, particularly from the point of view of their cost control systems.